DEPRESSION SMACKDOWN

REALITY-CHECK FIXED
WHAT MEDICATION, THERAPY,
AND LOVE FAILED

MEL. EDWARDS

Votre Vray, LLC
Indianapolis IN

If you seek to use any part of this book or my (Ms. Edwards) experience in other publications or media, or you seek to hire me to speak at your conferences and events, you may contact me via email at Mel@MsMelEdwards.com for such queries. I look forward to learning how I may assist your success with our mutual missions.

-Mel.

FREE BONUS

As an added bonus, if you go to my website www.MsMelEdwards.com and subscribe to my mailing list, you will not only get a monthly newsletter with at least one freebie and members-only offers and discounts, but also get a free download via email.

Remember: Action Builds Action

DISCLAIMER

Although this is a book of non-fiction, names and descriptions of all persons and locations, save for the author, have been altered. Any resemblance to actual people and places is purely coincidental. The purpose of the book is to show my journey alone while enlightening others about the world of major depressive disorder.

* * *

If you or anyone you know suffers from depression and is in crisis, please get help immediately. I am not a therapist, nor a doctor, and this book is in no way meant to diagnose, treat, or cure anyone. For assistance, find a qualified professional whose work and assistance you respect.

TRIGGER WARNING: Reading about someone else's depression may trigger emotional responses around depression or trauma memories. Take care of your health, and select or skip parts of this book to best support your own mental and emotional health.

Included below is the United States crisis hotline number.

Be safe and be well.

UNITED STATES SUICIDE PREVENTION HOTLINE
1-800-273-8255

CONTENTS

INTRODUCTION

In the middle of the night, when medical offices are closed, and you have already been to your general practitioner for assistance, where do you go when you are so ill that your inner voice begins to beg for relief -- even if that relief comes in the form of your last breath?

I went to a local emergency room, and before I knew it, a police officer told me he would not restrain me if I was cooperative, and he directed me into the back of his squad car. I am an American. I have no criminal history, and have had two parking tickets, one speeding ticket (which was expunged by attending driver's safety school for a day). This was not racial profiling. I am not homeless, or combative, and I did not have a weapon of any kind so the usual reasons we blame law enforcement for their protocol are not to blame.

I did not think this could happen to me in my country, and if it could occur to anyone, it certainly would not be part of the lives of those of us who tow the line, keep our noses clean, and give back to society on a routine basis. I was wrong.

As I gear up to share my truth, I admit that my heart is racing, my throat constricts, and I am clenching my jaw – the same jaw that created a stress fractured tooth in my sleep during the original events of this tale.

My inner voice says, "You don't have to do this." Perhaps. Then, I rationalize, "Don't tell. Keep it between us. You'll only cause them pain." This is the same voice that kept me silent for years. This voice, like an abuser, whispers shame, judgment, and false promises of protection in exchange for hiding my truth. I call this voice Same Shit Satan, as it repeats the same self-harming, negative messages each time it challenges me. No, I am not like a serial killer who will tell folks my dog told me to harm others. Instead, I fully realize that this is my own false-rationalizing voice. It is my fear, wrapped in honey tones and flannel blankets, inviting me to take a nap, quit my job, and wither in darkness. This voice is not my friend or my essential self. As one meme mentioned, "Your ego is not your amigo."

If you're searching for a phenomenal tale, meant for the big screen, you've chosen the wrong book. I haven't lived in a war zone, starved, been beaten, and left for dead. I haven't rescued hundreds from exile, trained a child to lead the world, been a combat veteran, or pulled anyone from a burning building. I'm just a normal woman who's lived with clinical depression. I'm worth as much as any person, just as fallible, and highly success-oriented. I have three degrees, several certifications and licenses, a family that loves me, and I am fully aware perfectionism is not reality. Just as no enduring atrocity created my disease, no piece of paper or accomplishment vaccinated me from it.

Clinical depression is real -- post-partum and otherwise. No celebrity sofa-hopper can deny it away, and I have dedicated the rest of my life to slaying this stigma dragon.

The first half of Depression Smackdown is my story down the rabbit hole, and back out again. The second half of the book is a presentation of resources and ideas to help those who love someone who is battling depression and/or anxiety. If you do not want to hear my story, skip it. No harm, no foul. My name is Mel Edwards, and I am a defeater of depression.

It is my hope this book will open discussion and save at least one life, if not many. Please talk to your loved ones if depression and anxiety are part of your life, or your family history. It may save someone else from beating his/herself up over it, and may open doors to reveal common ground.

Thank you for taking the time to read this. Spread the word that no one in this boat is alone. Slay the stigma and the silence, and uplift each other in strength and healing.

The light within me recognizes the light in you. Namaste

-Mel

PART ONE

MY STORY

SUNDAY BLUES

"Greif can't be shared. Everyone carries it alone. His own burden in his own way." -Anne Morrow Lindbergh

Major clinical depression, for me, did not come like a dark cloud that rises during a Sedona monsoon season, appearing on cue out of a sunny day, rolling in to dump despair on my life, and moving away as quickly as it materialized. Instead, it started as a surface crack that life picked at and pockmarked until the polish and joy was shaved from the surface letting the elements seep into the core, rotting the foundational timbers silently until the Sunday night when logic and practicality listened to Same Shit Satan calculate all the ways the struggle could end so I'd be free from conflict and shame, leaving someone else to say, "She told you she was in over her head."

Same Shit Satan is the negative voice that pops up when I'm overwhelmed. "You've always followed the rules. You've always been the good girl. What did it get you? The students who hate school and administrators who tell you if you were good at your job you'd un- school these kids and build them up into top performers. Nobody asked the kids, did they? You asked for help and were told you were a professional and you'd figure it out. Well, you must not be professional enough. Your career is over, anyway, after that screw up."

Have you ever watched someone's face change from joy to fear? Perhaps you've caught an actor going through the motions in a dramatic film, or watched your child try something they thought would be fun as the event became an uh-oh moment? Sunday blues

1

are nothing like that. At least, they aren't for me or anyone else I've watched slog through the day.

Imagine a slight dread, an "I don't wanna" moment, like getting up to work out on a cold dark morning, visiting that relative whose dogs have fleas and full reign of the living room furniture. Realizing it won't be life threatening doesn't make it more bearable to do, either. Knowing it is only going to be uncomfortable for an hour or two doesn't make you skip a step and shout for joy that you can do it.

Instead, it goes more like this:

"Are you okay?"

"Yeah."

"What's wrong?"

No answer.

"Can I help?"

Shakes head.

"Are you going to be okay?"

Shrug. "Yeah."

And so it goes for 12 hours or more winding up to Monday.

No outward anger surfaces on its own, except maybe the thud of objects hitting the table, doors slamming in protest, and accidentally spilled beverages combined with the desire for a nap only two hours after getting up for the day. The fighter isn't even in the ring most of the time. Instead, the sad-faced, soft-voiced Eeyore surfaces with a lot of shoulder glancing, half-hearted efforts, and no real reason to shout, scream or break china against the wall.

Most days, groceries are bought or laundry gets washed, folded, and put away. Meals are made and consumed in a lackluster assembly-line manner. Dishes are done, and everyone goes to bed, mostly hoping the one with the blues would get their shit together. Those are the good days.

At bedtime is when the real fun begins.

My head would hit the pillow for the night, after a mid-morning and mid-afternoon nap failed to revitalize me. By some grace, I count my breaths to three and I yawn. Every. Single. Time. Then, I begin counting again. Even on the ugly days, when everything makes me irate, I have never made it more than 30 breaths before succumbing to sleep. Often, ten or fewer deep breaths pass in or out before darkness and quiet move in, and my mind is suspended in time and space. When I'm really lucky, I don't dream for hours. On high-stress nights, the darkness is filled with anxiety dreams. My childhood anxiety dreams involved King Kong and Mighty Joe Young coming for me, though I loved and had compassion for both beasts by day.

When work was particularly stressful, I would clench my teeth, scream out loud enough to wake my husband, and thrash through foxholes on my imaginary but vivid journey through Hollywood-conjured world war battles.

This particular Sunday night has already become the embers of Monday morning.

Inside my head, I repeat, "I don't want to go. They don't care if I show up anyway. The kids hate school. Nobody does his homework. Mr. Wills won't punish them if they disrupt class. Ms. Sopa says, „Give kids a wide birth unless they disrupt, and disruptions won't be tolerated, but not to send them into the hall." In other words, she doesn't want to hear anything from me, or the students."

I think of the rowdiest kids, the ones who need the most help. "Johnsy won't ever be an Airborne Ranger if he won't follow any directions. Does he really think a commanding officer will tolerate him wadding up his orders and leaving them on the floor after Johnsy is dismissed?" My mind darts to the next student in need. "And Shakeena. The child still runs and plays tag in the hallway, squealing about cooties, and her mother told me, "My child don't act like that," as if I would make it up.

I never wanted to be a cop, the enforcer, or a babysitter! Why can't they be decent to each other? Why can't I find a job that pays as much as I make at this? My only option is retail. Minimum wage.

Then, my mind comes full circle again. "I don't want to go."

As the minutes tick away, that core statement brews a variety of unwholesome solutions.

What if I walked out the door right now, like the mother in that book my middle school kids read? She was in her nightgown, barefoot, and walked right out the back door into the cornfields. Her husband swore none of her clothing was gone. Her son wasn't sure, but he was certain he never heard her leave and he didn't understand why.

Petey (my dog) wouldn't understand.

My husband would be better off without me weighing him down.

Then Same Shit Satan begins to cheer me on, "Just get up, Mel, and start walking."

"I wonder what the temperature is?" I thought, knowing full well I wasn't moving, at least not yet.

I can't call a cab or walk down the street with a suitcase. Someone would see me. Then they'd look for me. They'd know I walked out, a big fat chicken.

I'm not afraid of kids, or teaching. I just fucking hate what it has become. The angry kids fighting with me and with each other, endless standardized tests, stupid politicians who can'" teach telling me

I can get any kid to be on grade level in one year regardless of the child's background, needs or abilities before they walked in my door, and that 70 freakin" percent of my pay should be based upon a faulty school report card system and one goddam test. Bastards.

My anger swells, and there is no room for reason, and no relief from the violence I feel toward being forced to do what my soul has told me for so long is wrong.

I listen to my husband and dog breathe in their slumber, and hope they don't wake up, don't know I'm ranting in my head, and do not realize that I am plotting my escape. I wish I'd planned ahead, bought a one- way train ticket with a fake I.D. and cash months ago. Or knew someone with a car who"d take a hundred bucks and never tell he drove me to Oklahoma or some other state no one I know lives.

"It'd backfire," I think. The ticket seller would remember me, or the driver would be arrested for murder because someone saw me in the passenger seat somewhere on the state line.

I should get a big coat, men's boots big enough for my shoes to slip inside and wear a weighted vest. Maybe someone would think I was a guy if I left in the night and they saw me head down, walking toward the next mill village.

I'd probably need a wig.

What if I got my hair cut real short, dyed it black, and wore a blonde wig until I made it to Louisiana or Texas? I could go into some lousy gas station, change my clothes, toss the wig and my disguise into the dumpster in back. Nobody would notice. I'm not that noticeable, and I don't know anyone in either of those states.

My mind races back to the job. "I don't want to go back there. I give up."

I have begged for help. Mrs. Freakin" Sopa said, "You're a professional. You'll figure it out." Didn't she know I've never, ever asked for help before? Couldn't she tell I was out of answers? I stared into the night and imagined her smug face, looking at me, without a word of help, or a single solution to keep me from drowning. I thought, "Thanks for nothing." So now, that's what I owe her, and Mr. Wills. Nothing. I'm never going back.

As the minutes tick by, I sink deeper into my loathing. "No one cares what I know as a professional, how I'd run things differently to actually help the students where they are. We're all a bunch of robots doing the same damned lesson on the same day so some idiot in an office can say, "Why don't you do as well as Mr. Wonderful? You ought to learn what he does. Then your students will do better." That's like telling a general, "You're both fighting in the same country, and you should win the same number of battles. It doesn't matter if your troops have typhoid and your territory requires you to fight in the bayou. If you're a good general, you'll get the same results as Captain Cool does on the planes on a cool March morning." Assholes.

When I've completely eviscerated my career, my supervisors and the political system the only other target at hand is myself.

I can't believe I waited so long to call Dr. Manny.

Then, I relive that exchange all over again, for at least the twelfth time. Repeated LASER-focused, self-flagellation is the name of the game with depression, if you don't know.

"Dr. Manny's office, may I help you?"

"I'm one of Dr. Manny's patients, but I haven't been there in two years. My depression is back and I think I need medication."

"Do you have a therapist?"

"I did, but I haven't tried to get in to her yet. I thought the medication should come first because it can take a while to help."

"Okay, well, Dr. Manny just had a quadruple by-pass, and we don't know when he'll be back in the office. Dr. Nash is booked for the next three months. Do you want to set an appointment for December?"

I tried to organize the information. "Three months?"

"I'm sorry, yes. Dr. Nash is doing double duty now. She's booked solid. I could put you on the cancelation list, but we may not know until the day of that there is an opening."

"Please."

"Sure. Let me get your information…"

I half laughed when I hung up. *"Thata girl, Mel. Finally get off your assets and ask for help, and your doctor is out on medical leave." Great.*

Asking for help has gotten you nowhere. Nice play, Shakespeare. First, Mrs. Sopa backed up by the lackluster Mr. Wills. Now, Dr. Manny cannot do a damn thing for you.

I looked up Julie's office and hit the button to make an appointment. Julie was my therapist last time, and I followed her from one office to another as she went into private practice. Julie would know what to do. To make an appointment with Angie, press 1; for Thomas, press 2, and so on the call went through number nine.

You've got to be kidding me. No Julie.

I pressed zero to leave a general message, "Um, Julie used to be my therapist. I was her client when she was back at the Crescent Health Center, and followed her there -- to her new office. I didn't hear her name on the list. I'm really depressed and I need someone to talk to. If she's not available, could someone else see me?"

I said my name and number very slowly and clearly twice. Then I hung up.

My throat tightened. My support system was broken. I expected Julie and Dr. Manny to be there forever. I loved the irony, since I was trying to figure out how to skip town.

For a moment, logic and clarity ruled. I calmed down briefly.

Of course they are not there, Mel. They're human. Remember, Julie's mom was sick. She probably retired to look after her.

Within seconds, I was back to pummeling myself. I shouldn't have signed my contract. I told my brother I didn't have it in me. Why did I let him talk me into teaching another year? Yes, I like kids and I believe they can do the work, but no one wants to. One told me yesterday he had better things to do with his life.

Why don't I have better things to do? Why can't I get help? I'm too tired to do it all.

The day I'd found out that Dr. Manny and Julie weren't going to do their professional magic to whip me back into shape I took an after-school nap and didn't budge when hubby got home.

"Are you sick?"

"Tired."

"Are you hungry?"

"No."

"Okay, I'll let you sleep."

I pulled the covers over my head and said nothing. No tears. No argument. One, breathe out. Two, breathe out, and so it went until I was asleep again.

All wasn't lost. Not really. The next day I got a message from Julie's office. I was right. She had retired, but she recommended this guy Saul at the Center. So I made an appointment with him for 6:30 p.m. on Friday. "Who the hell sees clients that late on Friday?" I wondered. "Apparently, Saul does." I snorted. Better call Saul. I thought of the TV show *Breaking Bad.* Was I going to be living in some TV spinoff about guys" unethical lawyers to make things happen for drug manufacturers? I giggled, and shook my head. At least I had some humor left.

When I met Saul, the therapist, on Friday night, I learned that he was about 10 years older than I am, and was a second-career counselor. He'd been a pianist for an orchestra that'd traveled with Broadway shows about twenty years earlier. He'd played for shows like *Evita* and *Cats,* knew a few stars, and had been on a few cast recordings. He asked me if he needed to call the police, if my depression was that bad. I told him no, but the truth was I was afraid to ask how bad someone had to be to need the police. I envisioned one of those lineup photos of someone with Don King hair, bloodshot eyes, flared nostrils, slouching for the shot wearing her stained, threadbare, flannel pajamas. For a woman who did not own a TV, most of my ideas about how others live come from the boob tube, or the silver screen.

By the time the intake appointment ended, Saul got my medical history and set my first normal appointment for Monday at 7 p.m.

Doesn't this guy have a life? I thought. I paid the receptionist and left.

Monday came and Saul gave me the explanation of several kinds of logical fallacies. I nodded as he talked about all-or-nothing thinking, circuitous thoughts, blaming, and so on.

I wanted to tell him I knew it all already. I used to be a debate coach for goodness sake, but I just accepted the handouts, nodded a lot, and when the time came I explained the crappiness of the teacher evaluation system, the injustice of passing kids on through social promotion to get them to high school even though they had not performed adequately since the 3rd grade.

He agreed with everything I said. The system sucked, and he also added other teachers he knew felt the same way. It felt nice to be supported for once.

"A kid isn't a test score," I said. "A test is a snapshot of a moment in time. Why should everyone pay a price because that snapshot is all the state wants to look at?"

Saul said I had every reason to be angry, and repeated what Julie had shared with me years ago. "Some believe depression is anger turned inward. Would you agree with that? That you're angry?"

I cried, "Of course I'm angry. It isn't fair. If a kid comes to me with an 80 IQ and gets from a 3rd grade reading capability to an 8th grade level in one year, that's HUGE, and the state department doesn't care. They compare that kid not to where he was in August, but to the previous graduating class. That doesn't make any sense."

Saul nodded and asked, "So why are you sick over it?"

I stopped crying, blew my nose and said, "I hate it. I hate forcing kids to take tests. I can't get them to behave because they hate English and the way I'm being forced to teach. I hate the way I'm being forced to teach from a script. My bosses won't help me, and parents are just as powerless as I am."

"I understand, and you have every right to be angry, but why are you sick?" Saul asked again.

I blinked repeatedly and thought, "I'm broken. I have nothing left to give. I don't want to do it anymore. If you offered me a bottle of poison to take right now so I wouldn't ever have to go back there, I'd take it, as long as you could promise me it'd just put me in the hospital for a little while --just enough time away to get a doctor to agree that I'm broken. I could quit, and I'd have proof. Proof that I'm not a failure, just broken. Broken can be fixed. Failure is forever."

That was the key. Right there. I *knew* in my gut that I was failing myself, my students, my legacy, everything. It did not matter that many students were learning, having some fun in class along the way, staying for extra help, and even thanking me for not letting them skate by without trying. I'd already judged myself harshly, and there was no appeal to redeem me, or my reputation, but I did not tell Saul. Instead, I shrugged. I was not ready to tell all my faults. I hoped it was just Same Shit Satan acting up again, but if you'd asked me, right then, who I blamed. I would have croaked, "Me," and there would have been no doubt that is what I believed.

Saul set my next appointment for Thursday. I'd never seen a therapist three times in a seven-day span before. Maybe I should've been worried, but I didn't care. He believed me, and that gave me reason to keep pushing until Thursday after work.

Thursday night he asked about some cognitive therapy homework I should have done. I had dashed it off five minutes before my appointment while sitting in my car in the parking lot, and the irony that I had become like some of my reluctant students was completely lost on me.

"How are you doing?" "Okay."

"Better? Worse? The same?" "Same, I guess."

"Did you get anything out of your last session that helped?"

I didn't tell him that we'd be writing argument papers in class already, and I'd used his cognitive therapy logical fallacies as a handout with my kids. I didn't tell my students that the handout was from my therapist, but explained that the logical mistakes could be used against someone in a written argument -- a key component to their Common Core curriculum.

The kids had loved it. Every single one of them had identified with at least one single logic breakdown, and a few boldly, unashamedly claimed them all. I told them that I, too, had some of the same logic challenges when assessing myself, and how I handled conflict. We laughed together, at our own thoughts, not each other.

It was October, and finally, I'd had a real conversation with all my classes instead of the dedicated students. No one got written up, disrupted, or pitched a fit. I even smiled when we talked, and more than one kid had come up to me after class that day and said they'd liked something about what we'd done that day. For a brief moment, I was a teacher again. I wasn't a disciplinarian, the enforcer, or the robot parroting out the party line about standardized testing. I'd missed the honesty so much that I cried when the last class left that day. *Maybe I wasn't a total failure,* I thought. *Maybe, I could do some of this canned curriculum, and still be the teacher I wanted to be…the teacher that loved the kids, as messy as their lives were, as much as they hated reading and writing, and helped them see their own dreams for their future selves.* I was exhausted, still, but I didn't go right to bed when I got home, and safely negotiated all the hours until my next session with Saul.

The problem was that I still had a tightrope to walk. When Saul asked me about the last few days, he was encouraged that I smiled when I mentioned a few of my students. Then, he asked again how the depression was, and what else I was angry about.

My breathing stopped briefly, and I swallowed. I knew to get better I'd have to share everything. The only way to heal was to relive my most shameful moment as an educator, the mistake that nearly cost me everything. The error that I still carried through my every waking moment, all the while fearing that someone else will learn I was unworthy of my position as an educator. The screw up was this:

The previous year I was teaching full-time days which, trust me, is a job and a half when you work with reluctant students. I was also trying to get out of debt and there was an opening for Night School instructors to work until 8 p.m. I applied and got the job. It was a case of hearing Same Shit Satan say, "You asked for it," as I put up with the baggage from a handful of students who had failed the same subject during the day, but were now in danger of never finishing high school. There was the young boy who talked about me in third person, refused to ask a direct question, and sauntered in and out with no paper, pencil or book, and was on probation academically, and legally. The girl who told me endlessly how gifted and talented she was and was always trying to get out of coming to class, even though the rules said clearly that day school was not an excuse to miss night school. The wanna-be soldier who couldn't put his cell phone away long enough to stay out of trouble even though he and his parents had signed the same contract everyone else had stating phones were absolutely not allowed. The resource student who needed resource-level assistance at night when there was none available.

There were a several good kids in class who simply wanted to understand enough to pass, and they're the ones who made it to the end of the course, and most of them learned new material, and even had a bit of fun, in spite of their past choices. I guess that phrase can be applied to me as well. By March I'd had enough of the same lame games and excuses from the "ne're do a thing" freeloaders, and I just wanted to respectfully make it through my night, make sure they each learned one new thing a day, and enjoyed having Friday through Sunday evenings free. Then "Ms. I'm Smarter-than-Everyone girl" pushed my buttons one time too many, and my affective filter gave out. She'd already missed too many classes, had required a call home about her attendance and lack of work, and now in the middle me explaining a passage that she was too cool to engage in, she started cutting jokes that she thought I was too deaf to hear. I stopped speaking, looked to her side of the room and said, "Quit fucking around."

Mr. Third-Person said, "Did she just cuss?"

The room froze. I turned to his side of the classroom and said, "Yes, I did. It is conduct unbecoming a teacher, and it won't happen again." Then, back to the other side I added, "But the message is clear. Cut it out." I apologized to the class as a whole, and most of the students said they understood, told me it is human to make a mistake, said they forgave me, and class continued without incident.

As soon as the period ended I went straight to a colleague and got my night boss's direct number. I left him a message about my screw-up, apologized, and then emailed Ms. Sopa. I also notified the second group of students of my mistake and told them if they didn't see me again, that I was relieved of duty. They were the good class -- the seniors looking to graduate in May -- and they tried really hard to tell me how it was okay, we all make mistakes, and how many other teachers they'd had done the same in the past and never apologized. I thanked them, said it was not okay to talk badly about my colleagues, and went about my lesson. The class went smoothly, and as soon as the students left, I tried to reach my boss again before clocking out for the night.

The next morning, Ms. Sopa summoned me. Because the night school director was not a highly qualified supervisor, but was working toward that credential, the school superintendent had gotten involved as next- in-line for this process. It was decided my day principal would handle the investigation.

"This is serious," Ms. Sopa said, as she stared at me, trying to make sure I was aware of the weight of the infraction.

"I understand," I said without elaborating.

"You can lose your positions, and your teaching license over this," she said as the reality twisted my larynx. "I was asked by the superintendent if this was a normal problem with you, and I said I didn't even know you knew such a word."

I stared at her, trying to not react for fear of breaking down. Weakness wouldn't help, nor excuses, even though I wanted to scream, "I told you I needed help with some of these kids. You told me I'd figure it out. Well, damn fine job I'm doing without your help." Instead, I stared and nodded, grateful I'd at least been given some benefit of the doubt.

"You're being put on paid leave while we investigate. I'll call you when a decision has been made. You are not allowed to call anyone or talk to anyone about this issue until you hear from me."

My heart skipped. This meeting was taking a turn down a path that sounded a lot like "You have the right to remain silent...".

She told me they'd handle plans for my classroom and I was to leave the building immediately, before anyone else saw me, and go directly home. She was probably giving advice more than orders, but she may as well hit me in the face with a two-by-four. I drove home replaying the conversation in my head, second guessing my every response, and wondering how I was going to live if I was never allowed to enter a classroom again. A monsoon was brewing, and started to drop the large splats of rain that signaled the oncoming deluge. I was afraid to go home because I didn't want to explain to my retired neighbor why I was there on a school day. I plotted to look up the street for her and vowed to keep driving by the cross street if she was on the porch. Fortunately, it was still early enough that she wasn't out drinking her glass filled with instant coffee, so I pulled in and rushed into the house, dropped my school bag in the corner, took off my professional attire, hanging it neatly in the closet, put on my nightshirt, stared into space, and slowly melted on top of my bed.

Satan piped up, "Now what the hell are you going to do, Ms. Potty Mouth? Who the hell will hire a failure of a teacher for what your professional level pay brings in? Teachers may not make much, but it sure is more than retail or fast-food provides. You might as well practice, 'Would you like fries with that?' you loser."

I spent the day alone at home, pacing, attempting to nap, and wasting time as I tried to avoid going into a meltdown or panic. My husband was at work, and knew about the infraction, but not the outcome. Although he has never been mean to me, I knew he'd be disappointed that I'd put our finances in jeopardy, not only for the present, but possibly for many years to come. How would I face him?

Fortunately, when he came home that night, and I had explained everything the best I could, he assured me that he was concerned, but he was also aware of how I'd been burning the candle at both ends for awhile, and that it was a human mistake. Unfortunately, where I was teaching, it seemed that teachers were not allowed to be human. Students and their parents could throw things, cuss everyone out, threaten law suits, and behave in a generally deplorable manner on a regular basis, but one f-bomb was all it took to remove decades of a teacher's excellent reviews, conduct, and results. In short, teachers are expendable, and held to a level of conduct higher than the president of the United States, and that was before we started being evaluated based upon student test scores.

The next afternoon I heard from Ms. Sopa. "I need you to come in early tomorrow. Can you be here at 7 a.m.?"

"Yes."

"You'll be teaching, so be ready."

"Okay. Thank you," I said coolly, but hung up and cried my eyes raw. I still had a job. Thank G-d. I still had a job. I wasn't fired.

Damn. That means I still have to teach that kid who hates school and would just as soon spit at me as look at me. Satan added, "Isn't that cute? Even when you win, you lose. Suck it up, Buttercup, and put on your happy face. You may not be good enough to do what your boss, and the world expects of you, but you're better than nothing."

When I arrived the next morning, I went into the principal's office, and she shut the door. "This is a very serious matter."

It was déjà vu. "I understand," I said, and swallowed hard as she directed me to sit down.

"We investigated, and everything you said seems to be true."

I assumed that meant that she knew that what I said, that I apologized, who I said it to, and that it had only been once, but I was too afraid to ask. She certainly did not sound like she was glad about any of this - even the outcome.

"I have two copies of a letter here that states what you've told me, and the result of our findings -- that you chose to use profanity in the classroom. One copy will remain on file and one copy is for you. Signing it does not admit any other guilt or problems. It is just a verification of what you reported to us, and that we followed up. I need you to sign now."

I felt like I needed a lawyer, or at least a union rep in the room with me, but our school had neither. Time seemed slower as she handed me the pen. I put my perfectly shaped signature at the bottom of the page, and slid the pen and paper back toward her across the desk.

"This remains between us, and should not be brought up again. As long as it never impacts your day job, you can remain certified. You will not be paid for the nights you missed, but will return to work on Monday."

"I am still teaching nights?"

"Yes, you're needed and your supervisor spoke well of your work there, too. However, should this happen again, you can expect to be relived of your duties, and license. Do you understand?"

I half-expected to hear a gavel come down hard. "Yes."

"Good. You've got a lot to do to get ready for today," she said, in an effort to dismiss me.

I stayed in the chair, and she tilted her head in confusion. I asked, "Will you tell anyone?"

"Not unless I have a reason to."

What did that mean? "But, if I were to apply elsewhere, would you tell someone that if you were a reference?"

"I would say there was one incident that was cause for concern, but that it was an anomaly, and quite a surprise, but it was handled quickly, and appropriately, and has not occurred again, if that is the case."

Satan said, "You're screwed. She's going to tell everyone. Your career is over after all."

I thanked the principal, got up, wished her a good day, grabbed my copy of the condemnation letter, opened the door, and headed out into the silent hallway. The meeting had taken less than five minutes, which I supposed was appropriate since my infraction had taken even less than that. Satan added, "Twenty years of professionalism gone in one swoop. You're a real pro - even at fucking up."

I folded the letter, slid it into my laptop bag, and headed to my classroom. I was back, and now I was going to have to find the energy to be a teacher when I just wanted to go home, curl into a ball, and dissolve into dust. At that moment I'd deemed myself an utter failure as a teacher, and vowed to resign at the end of the school year, never seeking to be a public school teacher again.

Depression does that. It makes mountain ranges out of solitary mountains, even after you've reached the peak and planted the flag, tattered from battle.

I'd like to say the semester ended with a bang, that I got myself together, vanquished Same Shit Satan, and moved onward with my career. Instead, he grew stronger, emboldened by my weakness. The negative self-talk continued. Even though I now look back and see that I was exhausted and battling normal fatigue the reality is that at the time, I felt it was my own weakness growing (much like a child's fear of the monster in the dark). I was sure everyone knew my shameful moment, and that I would wear a scarlet letter F on my chest for the rest of my life.

My vision of myself was marred, and the good that happened paled by the monolithic mistake that had nearly cost me my livelihood. I was not truly able to see what I was doing correctly. This skewed vision carried into my daily life, and I could no loner see or hear the good that I was doing as anything more substantial than mere grains of sand compared to the boulder of shame I was carrying around with me. I did not know how to set down my mistake and move onward.

You see, I was always the good girl, the one who followed all the rules; I should have known better, and yet, I'd still screw myself because I let my anger at Ms. Smarty-Pants get under my skin. I was letting her negativity toward school, and my position, take me down to her level -- heck, even below it -- and I had no idea where to turn.

A few weeks later, when contracts for the following school year came out I told my brother-in-arms that I wasn't going to sign it and return to teach anymore. He knew of my incident, and, like me, was not a native of the area where we worked. We'd had many frank discussions so when he told me not to give up, that he thought I had a gift as a teacher, that next year would be better after I had the summer off and got some rest, I signed my contract.

Basically, I ignored my intuition that said I was too vulnerable, and that I needed to look at using my skills elsewhere. I chalked up that self- protective voice to the same stinkin' thinkin' voice of Same Shit Satan. I repeated my brother's words to myself and said, "Rest for the summer. Next year will be different," and drove away at the end of the year filled with apprehension and doubt nevertheless.

For me, what had changed in my life from the first year at my position was I"d been given some of the least motivated students in the school, and changed from teaching upper classmen to freshmen. That may not seem like much of a difference to an outsider, but realize about 30% of freshmen were not making it to their sophomore on time at my school because they were either not ready or willing to do the work that was required of sophomores. As a result, I went from teaching the barely- prepared to others who had not passed a class since they were in 5th grade. Those non-performing students had been socially promoted for the past three years through middle school. (*Socially promoted means, they were moved along with their peer group even though they had demonstrated no proficiency or aptitude of any kind in some or all of their courses.*) Of course socially promoted students were not set up for success. They knew it. I knew it. However, the rule-makers did not care, and they fully believed I should be able to magically reach out to every student, no matter how low their proficiency or prior performance, and bring them up the 10th grade preparedness in one semester, or one full year if they were also in the remedial reading course. In other words, one teacher was expected to do what three years of education (or more) had not, and we were reminded regularly our future pay would be based upon what our students earned on their end of the year state examination in my subject area.

The problem was no one in charge ever asked the kids how to help them, or had a special meeting with the students and their parents laying out the whole truth of what the kids were up against. There was no buy-in from the kids or their families, and I did my best, which got most of my students to the 8th grade level or higher, and over 80% of them up to grade-level in the little time we had together. It was hard, hard work filled with anger and frustration coming from them and, in the end, it broke me down.

This is not to say that there were no victories along the way. The wonderful team of teachers in my department had worked like mad to help our students reach levels that even our administrators were surprised by, even if those levels were not the 100% they'd been charged with expecting of us, and our students. By May, several students who had not performed all year finally had a seemingly miraculous burst of personal insight and realized that "no work" really did mean "no grade" and they'd be left behind for the first time in their lives. Most got themselves together enough to pass, even if it was by the skin of their teeth.

What could I have done to stay out of the dungeon of depression? I now know I should have had more "me" time to rejuvenate, reflect, refresh, and renew myself for each day long before I took on the night school job in addition to my day job. Instead, I got to work early, worked extra-late, and used much of my evenings and weekends digging through every resource I could get my eyes or hands on to help fix their challenges. My well of resources for the classroom was deep, but for my own health? That water had dried down to the bedrock, obviously, and no summer break was going to magically fix that. My joyful nature, creative soul, and spirit of success had been shaved down to the shaft. I, the teacher who worked so tirelessly for the success of others, had failed myself in the most basic sense of the word, partly due to my poor health choices, but I would not realize it until I was under lock and key, against my will.

THE PLAN

"Depression is the most unpleasant thing I have ever experienced...It is the absence of being able to envision that you will ever be cheerful again." - J.K. Rowling

In spite of protests and begging from my colleagues, and my night supervisor -- even after my moment of shame -- I was savvy and healthy enough not to re-up as a night school teacher. I finally realized that when one does work solely for money one earns every penny, much like the people who marry for security. However, heading into summer break, my transgression was still weighing on me enough that I did not dare to breathe wrong for fear of losing two decades worth of credentials and experience. Besides, spending five hours a day doing the "please behave and do your work" song-and-dance was draining enough on a good day.

To say my summer was lackluster is putting it mildly. I went into a type of hibernation, except I lived in air conditioned comfort, left the house only when necessary, gave up all exercise, started eating the lowest nutritional value products I could get my hands on and slept more than not. I put on ten pounds in a month, gave up wearing make-up, did not buy any new back-to-school clothes or do anything to get myself out of my hole. I was bereft of energy, and most feeling. Nothing made me smile, and if emotions did come they were vile, hateful internal rages that made me so upset I could not even stand being alone with myself. I was in mourning, for life "before": before my error, before when my friends and I worked out together, before I had students I was not allowed to help in a way that I knew worked, before I taught a canned curriculum. My eyes only looked backward, and the only person I could lash out at was myself.

I did not garden, create art, exercise, sing, hang out with friends, have sex, try anything new or get help. Looking back, I can honestly say it was a type of slow suicide-in-progress. I banked on the fact that my husband worked year round as my ticket to do as little as possible. Although I was angry at the system, I was still most mad at myself for the screw-up, and my unwillingness to ever have to explain that mistake was also taking my will to do anything else. I was certain that if my colleagues knew about my mistake they'd build a Salem witch trial fire to rid me from their ranks.

Yet, when the school year began, I put on a reasonably professional face and managed to get through the rest of the school year by some cosmic grace. I was not strong enough to face any challenges because I had not cared for myself, refilled my reserves, or built a support system. I thought that if I kept my head down and mouth shut that I'd somehow muddle through.

Within the first month of the new school year I learned not one or two, but a full half of one class of students had not passed a single course in three years before landing in my classroom, three additional students had always been in small-group, self-contained special education classes to help them focus and succeed, and everything I'd planned to teach in the fall semester had to be thrown out the window because a district leader had a different curriculum we'd be required to follow.

Why could I not get anyone to hear that our school's idea of shoving ill-prepared children into 90 minute reading classes, a subject they were not only weak in but also hated, was not motivational or inspirational on any level, and no amount of sleight of hand was going to change that? Was it all a numbers game to them? Were their students and teachers only notches in their respective belts? Or were they also drowning in their own sea of unreasonable situations and expectations?

Instead of assistance, respect and support, my colleagues and I endured another stern reminder that the school report card system was not only rating the school as a whole, but that the rating had a large part to do with how my students performed on a standardized test -- the same testing system that most had never passed before at any prior point in their educational careers. Teachers were told to figure out how to throw our educator fairy dust around enough to create the miracle that would bring our children to the promised land of passing without classroom aides, parent input, or additional funding for resources.

Instead, the en vogue best practice was to force my team members and I to teach the same subject, largely the same way, on the same day, and give the same assessments to all students to figure out how to troubleshoot their testing skills before the big statewide exam. Although we were told that our curriculum was NOT a script, we were simultaneously directed to plan our lessons together, have a large percentage of our assessments be identical across the grade level between educators, cut out anything that was not absolutely necessary, and revisit test prep skills as often as possible. If that was not a script, in their estimation, I did not desire to know what was.

I was doubly disheartened. Sure, master teachers will spout platitudes and rosy agreement to whatever administration wants only to return to the classroom and teach their own way once the doors were closed, but that could not quite fly in my school. We were all observed by four principals, a curriculum supervisor, and district official each and every quarter of the school year - all unplanned and unannounced. In other words, Big Brother was watching, again and again.

Our lesson and unit plans had to be available by the classroom door so that any observer could waltz in, check up on us, evaluate if we were doing what we said we would in the manner our group had outlined in curriculum meetings, quickly moving onward. Administrators said it was to help us if we were weak in a specific area and to high light our skills to our colleagues, but I knew of three different teachers in my subject area in another local school whose contracts had not been renewed when their teaching expertise had been lauded previously. It felt like the system was pitting us against one another, and none of us were happy. One new teacher from a nearby school actually went home one weekend, disconnected his number, moved, and never returned to teaching. Did no one notice that was a red flag?

Interestingly, in an effort to show how proud they were of some of our work, the district was having teachers from other schools come and watch how we were doing things to see if their faculty could learn from our methods. It made me feel like the Kiss-up Kid, and I hated showing how fantastic my canned methods were when I wasn't permitted to use other topics, techniques or resources that my colleagues were not also using. I wondered, as I looked at myself in the mirror, if the word "liar" would rise up out of my forehead for the entire world to see? I wanted desperately to ask the district visitors "Are you guys being forced to do this, too? Are you okay? Does anyone ever tell you what you do right?"

Rumors swirled. If instructors were not in step, they were being reviewed quite harshly. It was even recommended to some that they begin looking for a future beyond the classroom. There was no mentoring except to be told to act like "so-and-so." The only mention or bolstering of our good works came when a teacher led in a sporting championship or raised enough funds on his/her own to do a special event that made the district look good, and no mention was made that all the things that had made each teacher uniquely successful in the past were no longer welcome in any classroom (as they were now against the Common Core, district visions, and team consensus). My joy in the teaching process was gone, not only because I was still ashamed of my error, but now because I knew, in the depths of my body and soul, that no child was a test score, and no educator shines reading from a script written in someone else's voice. The bottom line was the business model had come to education, and I wanted nothing to do with it, let alone to be forced to carry the standard into battle.

Administration spouted to the press and parents that we were a high- rigor magnet school, but removed all creative arts from core classes, belied any teacher-led instruction, and shunned guest speakers in exchange for student-centered instruction from non-fiction texts. Someone somewhere wanted assembly-line education that would produce passing test scores with the misguided vision that this would make children strong in STEM and put a feather in the district's cap, and every administrator in the district was drumming it into our lives. It made me sick, quite truly, in every sense of the word. That's when I'd finally made the call to Dr. Manny, and Julie, only to find out they were not available to me any longer. I should have been more grateful for Saul.

By October my peers and I were trying to keep our heads above water as we struggled to get ill-prepared children interested in learning material we barely cared about. I did sneak in lessons on fencing with foam swords when we read part of *The Tragedy of Romeo and Juliet*, as we were not given time to read the entire play. My classes worked with a visiting actor for a few hours to tackle poetry with limited success because my students were big on bravado, but low on true confidence. The time I would have had in the past to boost them one-on-one was slashed from the calendar, and we trudged onward from topic to topic under broad thematic umbrellas thought up during the summer by a few chosen teachers. Instead of counting my tiny victories, I regularly inventoried my failures. I blamed the district, my administration, myself, and the parents who never returned my calls for the state the classroom, but each night as I suffered night terrors, insomnia and nightmares, I paid dearest.

On average, each class had between two and ten outbursts per day as combative students vied for attention any way they could get it because they were unable or unwilling to do any of the most-basic work set before them, no matter how carefully I'd sifted through the mandates to individualize, sugar-coat, and scaffold the heights they were being asked to reach. One girl proudly announced that the year before she'd been referred to the office every day, and she wondered why I had not kicked her out that often because she clearly was acting out. I told her it was clear she was trying to leave, and she was not in school to visit the office all day. The whole truth was I did not feel supported enough to send her to anyone anyway. I felt utterly alone.

I did not have the heart to admit aloud to anyone that my grade-level administrator was not doing his job in a way that benefitted me or changed their behavior, not that I would have ever said so to a student anyway. The vice-principal was a teddy bear of a man who spent much time listening and nodding, with an occasional punctuated sigh as he would tell them to go back to class and not do it again. Short of violence, there was nothing they could do to each other, or me for that matter, in my room that warranted even assigning detention to the kids, and ironically, I was on detention duty which meant if they got assigned the time, I had to be the enforcer, yet again. Instead, I was asked repeatedly if I'd called home first, and told he had other things to do than to speak to my students about how their behavior impacted others. How he expected me to stop class, confidentially call home, and keep teaching all at once is beyond me. I knew, though, that it was time to give up counting on him to enforce the rules, including the ones he had made about wearing their IDs, sticking to dress code, and what constituted appropriate school conduct. I began spending nearly all of my planning time each day calling home and writing emails to those parents that I could not reach any other way sharing my sugar-coated concerns for my non-performing students.

I compared notes with other instructors in my wing and nearly 30 students in their freshman year were failing every class, refusing to do any homework, and acting up, but Mr. Wills just sighed and shook his head. One teacher joked about needing a drink. Another said he was working 80-hour weeks trying to get ahead. One coach gave up grading and lesson-planning completely and used only the canned curriculum because she was too defeated to put forth any further effort after she was written up for a child having her feet up on the desk during class. Frankly, I felt that there was no hope to be found.

The hardest day of the week for me was not a teaching day. It was Sunday because as the hours passed my mind would race, and swirl with the laundry list of all that had gone wrong in class so far, the humiliation of last spring's mistake, and how many things could go wrong with the coming week. Like the Shel Silverstein poem where the child lists all that is wrong with her health and how she could not possibly go to school mirrored my thoughts, except there was no miraculous revelation that it was the weekend at the end of my mental process. Every week I got more depressed, in spite of Saul's three-times a week sessions with me, and my general practitioner's solution -- a prescription for Cymbalta -- was not helping.

After my beloved husband went to bed each night, Same Shit Satan bolstered my mental lashing and continued on as I tossed on

29

the sofa. "I don't want to go back there. I can't do it. I can't make them behave. The kids don't want to be there. Administration could care less if I ripped my heart open right in front of them. The at-risk kids are so angry at everyone, and who can blame them? I hate it. Please, I'll do anything to not go back. Don't make me," I thought. Then, the darkness offered, "Too bad you're not suicidal."

The thought of death, for the first time in my life, sounded not like a punishment, but instead, like relief. I was exhausted. Again, I said, "I really would do just about anything," and there was no remorse in that truth.

The proverbial logical angel on my shoulder said, "You have insurance. Go to the hospital. You're depressed. See if there is something else you can take."

I began to think of how I would take my own life, if I really wanted to die, while metaphorically patting myself on the back for each method I could dismiss.

"I can't shoot myself. I don't own a gun." Thank goodness. Besides, that would be a terrible mess for my husband to clean up, and the gunshot would wake the neighbors.

"I hear if you take a bunch of pills, you just vomit them. Besides, the deadliest pill I have is Tylenol, and I doubt I have enough to shut down my kidneys," I thought, even though I had no idea how much that would take.

"What about hypothermia? I'd have to walk away in light clothing with no coat and probably no shoes, and someone is bound to see me. They'd know I was a coward trying to run away from my problems, and the gravel in the road would really hurt my feet." The shame of being found out was worse than the pain of going to work, and my pansy attitude about pain certainly kept me from being willing. Of course a suicidal person would not worry about that. I just needed medication that worked.

I recalled a friend in middle school once said she'd get in a warm bath full of sharp razor blades because it wouldn't sting and she could just bleed to death. Twenty-something years later the image still made me want to vomit. I guess that leaves hanging," I thought, "but where?" When my pet rabbit had been put down her bladder had let lose, and since we were trying to sell our house so we could move away, that wouldn't be good for the resale value.

My life insurance would be more than enough to pay off all my debts. My husband could do as much or as little as he wanted once I was gone, I reasoned. He'd be debt-free, too.

My mind circled through the possibilities again, going back to simply walking out the door with no identification -never to be seen again. I'd read a book like that with middle school students, where a woman walked off into the field behind her house while her husband and son slept. At the time I'd interpreted her departure as escape from domestic violence. What if she'd just hated her life?

"I don't hate my life," logic said. "I just hate my job."

I silently wept, "You're the idiot who signed your contract. Now what are you going to do about it?"

I sat up and stared into the moonlit living room. Hubby was sleeping, and probably sick of my Eeyore-attitude. Even Petey, my rescued toy poodle who was usually so stuck to me that I'd nicknamed him Velcro- dog, did not even notice I was missing from the bedroom.

I looked at my phone. I'd been berating myself for hours. It was just past 3 a.m.. If I was going to do something, it needed to happen soon, before someone stopped me.

"What do you want?" my mind asked.

"Darkness," I answered myself. That wasn't quite right, though. "I want everyone to leave me alone. I can't sleep. I can't go back there. Not like this. I'm useless."

The tears came hot and hard. "I can't face anyone. I used to think I was a good teacher. I'm not. Good teachers don't have kids act out in class. They have their shit together." I shuddered. *Don't make me go back. Don't make me. Please, please. Please...*

I blew my nose and dug my purse out of my school bag. I needed help. I didn't want to wake my husband. He needed his sleep, and had to be to work by 7 a.m. One of us had to be able to pay the bills.

I pulled out my wallet, slipped my insurance card and driver's license from their sleeves, and stared at them. My driver's license had a picture of me when I used to be a runner with my friends and former co- teachers. I missed them. They were mothers now, and I had only birthed my own misery.

As I stared at my photo, I wondered, "What have I done? I was beautiful and happy and now..."

I was fifty pound fatter, unable to teach, broke and ashamed of my mistakes, my weakness, and my life. I once wanted a baby, too, a little boy. I dreamt of him once. He was blonde with blue eyes and was named Liam.

I looked up to the sky as my tears continued. Stargazing is what the vet had called it when our pet rabbit was gasping for life and breath. It was a sign, she said, that the rabbit was dying. Here I was feeling like she looked. I could not breathe, but the snot and tears did not stop. I felt the former beauty of my heart and soul slipping away, unable to bear my piteous state.

"I have a necktie," I thought. "I could let myself into the shed, and hang myself there." I knew my husband never went in the shed, and there was no floor, just the earth. Anything that leaked out of my body after the last breath would wash away with the garden hose. It would not ruin the house sale -- something I assumed he'd do to not have to live where I'd died.

Then, I imagined the neighbors talking. They'd stand around and go on about how they never knew, and look at my husband and shake their heads. I thought of my mother, and knew she'd be even more disappointed in me, and heard my father say, "No parent should have to bury a child," like he did when a girl my brother had known died in a sporting accident.

I looked back to my ID and insurance card, and reasoned that I didn't really want to die. If I had wanted to, I would have done something. I needed help. *Please, someone help me*, I thought, as I pulled on a pair of jeans and my sneakers. I was still braless, in my nightshirt, and I left my husband a note that I was going to the hospital, grabbed my car keys and headed out the door. I did not take my phone or anything else with me because if I did not make it to the hospital, I did not want anyone to find me, at least, not today.

Even though our house was fairly near one of the local hospitals, I drove past the turn and headed to the facility where I'd had my emergency hysterectomy several years earlier. Even though I'm not Catholic, they were nice to me there. One nurse even held my hand and prayed for me before surgery regardless of the fact I was not her faith. Short of having my mom rock me in her arms until the world disappeared, I could think of no other safe place to be at the moment.

As I got on the highway, I thought, "What if I just kept driving?" "They'd never stop looking," Logic assured.

"Why? Why do I have to go back there? I hate it. I hate being a failure. I don't want to be a teacher. Not like that," I screamed inside my head. I was still railing against going to work in a few hours. I truly had not ruled it out. I had no backup plan. I figured some doctor at the ER would give me some kind of shot for anxiety and I'd calm down, but I did not know. The only thing I was certain of was that Cymbalta was not helping and I was so, so tired.

As I pulled into the hospital parking lot, it was still dark outside, but the faint tinges of daylight were showing in the brighter blue star-filled haze. "Help me, please." I thought as I walked to the emergency room door. "Please, help me."

The doors slid open to reveal an empty waiting room. I stood looking for what to do. Once I spied a young woman, I walked up to her desk and said, "I need to see a doctor. I'm depressed. My medication is not working."

The girl asked me to sit and asked for my information. I shoved my ID cards at her and sat silently.

After she typed it all in, verified that I was the same woman who had the hysterectomy and the annual mammograms, and that I still worked for the local school district. I nodded as I picked up my cards and slid them in my back pocket. She asked about my medication and I pulled my prescription bottle out of my pocket. At least I'd had the presence of mind to bring it with me.

"How long have you been on this medication?" she asked.

"Three weeks." I added, "I don't think it works, or it isn't working yet."

She nodded and kept typing. "Okay," she handed it back to me. "Have a seat and someone will call for you in a minute."

I sat alone, counting my breaths, trying to not run out the door, get in my car and run head on to the nearest wall to get the pain over with. I wondered if my husband or dog knew I was gone yet. I wished I had my phone so I could check the time.

I don't believe I'd sat there more than fifteen minutes when the triage nurse called my name. As I walked toward her I looked toward a window and saw that the sun had come peeking through the trees. At least I wasn't crying anymore. I had gone numb.

EMERGENCY

I followed the triage nurse into a cubby-sized office. She offered me a seat between the wall and her desk as she shut the door, and said, "So, I understand you have depression."

Without provocation, my eyes welled up and I nodded.

She verified my identity, handled all the questions about my insurance, and said they'd run some tests and I could put my personal affects into a hospital branded white plastic bag. She took my pulse and temperature, and checked my blood pressure.

"Okay, let's bring you down the hall to a room."

My tears abated as I walked down the hall and she led me to the left of the hall, just past the nurses" station. There was a cart in the far right corner and a bed in the left.

"Have a seat. I'll get you a gown and you can get changed."

She returned quite quickly, handed me the gown and said, "Put this on and your clothes can go under the bed. I'll keep your bag with me so your belongings are secure while you go through testing. Open the door when you're dressed, and the nurse will be in."

She closed the door behind her and left the room. I got up and began to change. I noticed there was a large window by the bed, but it was covered. I pulled off my nightshirt and jeans, and put the gown on, surprised to find even though it was meant to be open in the back, that it wrapped around me easily and left nothing to the breeze.

I opened the door, walked to the bed, boosted myself back upon it, socks still on and lie down. Finally, I felt like I could relax and I closed my eyes until I heard a gentle knock on the open door.

"Hi, Mel. I'm Susan. I'll be taking care of you today."

I sat up and looked at the forty-something woman in front of me with blonde hair and glasses. She was calm, and explained that I needed to go down the hall and pee in a cup, but because I was depressed, I would need to leave the door cracked open and she'd stand outside and wait.

Did she think I was going to the hospital to kill myself? Certainly, if I'd wanted to do it, I would have done it. The truth was that I did NOT want to die. I only wanted my pain to end, and to find hope again -- someday.

"Okay," she said, "Let's go." She entered the hall, stopped briefly to grab a cup for my urinalysis, and smiled softly as she handed it to me. "The bathroom is just down the hall around the corner."

I went ahead of her, found it, and entered, leaving the door open a crack, wondering if I'd have any pee left in me after all the tears, but I had no problem meeting the requirement. The bathroom was pristine and I was not concerned or afraid of what the rest of the ER visit would entail, but I would soon learn that protocol was nothing like going in for a broken arm, the flu or any other mundane emergency needs case.

> ### *20/20 Vision*
>
> If you have received any type of rudimentary education in suicide prevention, you have probably been told that you should call for emergency help (9-1-1 in America) if you are feeling suicidal or if someone you love has stated they have a plan to kill themselves. I am not disputing this call to action. However, do you know what happens once you call? There are different laws and facilities available to the mentally ill in each nation, state and community. For most of us, knowing those laws and facilities does not matter. What matters is saving a life, if possible.

After I handed her the cup, she redirected me to my room and said she'd be right with me.

When she returned, she stood just inside the doorway and said, "Have you ever come to the hospital for depression before?"

I shook my head. "No," I croaked, and swallowed. "I bet you could use some water."

"Yes, please."

"Okay, let me get that for you and I'll explain how things work."

My heart rate quickened slightly as I waited for her to return, and the words hung in the air. How things work sounded serious.

Susan entered, and held out a miniature bottle of water. "Here you go," she said.

I opened it and took a drink while she waited, and when I put the top back on she again gave me that soft smile.

"Because you're suicidal, I need to take everything out of the room. We do not have a mental health ward here. The charge nurse will have to call around to try to find you a local room."

I held my breath.

"You cannot leave this room without supervision. If you try to go home, we will have to call the police to come and get you, and bring you back. I do not know if a room is available in a local facility or not, but until one is, this is where you will stay."

She paused and looked at me. "Do you understand?" I swallowed hard, and replied, "Yes."

"There is a doctor on call, and office hours start soon. If he can, he'll be in to see you before he goes to the office. Otherwise, it may be tonight before he can see you."

My head spun, but I kept my thoughts to myself, "Tonight?! I have to go to work. I have a job. My husband doesn't know where I am!"

"Okay, I am going to empty the room now. Do you need anything before I start?"

I must have replied, because she began unplugging things, moving out an IV tree, the cart from the corner, even the plastic resin chair.

I thought, "The chair?! What the hell am I going to do with the chair?" as I stared at the white walls resigned to wait for the doctor, and hoping he could come in before his office day began.

The room was empty now, and there was nothing to do but lie back down. Susan came to the door and asked if I'd like the light off.

"Yes, please," I said, and she flicked the switch and left the door wide open.

I got under the waffle weave blanket and sheet and placed my head on the pillow, with my face to the wall. "Great," I thought. "I guess I am not going to work today. They'll figure it out. They would have to if I'd crashed my car," I reasoned. "No big deal. The kids would be happy to have a sub."

Then Same Shit Satan came in for the one-two punch, "Nice job. Now what? Every man for himself? They can't count on me at school. My husband doesn't know where I am. I'm a failure. I'm a useless wife, a terrible teacher, and so much for being the daughter with all the education."

I must have fallen asleep because I woke to the tapping on the door. It was a male, and he said he was working on getting me a room somewhere. He said the doctor was on his way, and he'd let me know if he could find a room. Then he added, "If there is no room available, you may have to stay here a while."

He looked at my face and added, "It could be as late as Thursday before one opens up, but hopefully not. I'll let you know."

I gulped. "Thursday?! It was Monday. I might have to wait in this room until Thursday?" I screamed inside as my face twisted and I clamped my lips together. "What have I done? I just wanted medicine. Can't they just give me a shot to sleep and send me home? Can't someone come get me?"

I was wiping my nose on a tissue left behind and smirked to myself. "They took out the chair, but goodness knows the paper cut I could give myself on this damned tissue box. Stupid bastards."

I looked at the faux window again, this time with suspicion and wondered if they really could observe me through it. I made a face at my reflection and lie back down, this time slowly rocking myself hearing my mother's soft toning that she always did as she rocked me. "Ah ah ah, ah ah, ah ah aaaaah," as she had cradled me through many an illness. I was more ashamed than ever as I realized the mess I was in. I was unable to get my shit together, and here I was trapped in a hospital room, waiting to be sent somewhere else for treatment. "I'm sorry, Mom. I'm so sorry I couldn't do it anymore. I'm sorry I screwed up, and I love you," I thought as my nose and eyes ran. So this was it was like to be a failure, incompetent, and useless. I was no better than the lowest of the low, and I began to realize that I might never get better. "At least Van Gogh could paint," I told myself, and I closed my eyes and tried to remember to breathe.

* * *

When there is no clock, phone, or classroom bells counting hours for me, I lose track of time quite easily, and this morning was no different. The more I thought about my failure as a teacher, the easier it was to let that loathing ooze into my personal life.

"I should have walked out the door and kept going." "My husband would be better off without me."

"I'm a train wreck."

"I'm useless."

Then, in walked my Angel. Not a divine revelation, a marital one. My husband was at the door, came to my bedside, and took my hand.

I immediately choked down my sobs and tried to apologize. "I'm sorry. I'm so sorry. I just can't…"

He cut me off. "It's okay," he said and hugged me.

That's when I felt weakest of all, surrounded by his strength and concern. My Saran Wrap shield melted as he hugged me. I shook in his arms and he stroked my hair. He told me not to be sorry. It was not his first experience with mental illness, or hospitals, or a loved one who could not cope. He treated me with the dignity anyone would have wished for, and it was my little miracle for the moment.

I asked how he found me, knowing full well the note I'd left him only stated that I was going to the hospital, and not to which one.

"I called around until I found you were here. Then I came over."

"You didn't go to work."

"I called in."

"You didn't have to do that."

"Yes. I needed to know you were okay. Oh, and Pam called from work. They didn't know where you were. I told her you were in the hospital, but that's all I could say."

I looked down at the blanket avoiding his eyes and discussing work. All I knew was that I didn't want to go back there to be talked to like garbage by the students who didn't want to be there either. I didn't have the backbone anymore to stand up to their misdirected and toxic anger, or to tell my boss, again, that I needed help reaching these students. It was crystal clear to me that I was at the end of my usefulness in that position. Anyone could do better.

"Hey?" my Angel nudged me. "What's going on?"

"They are trying to find a room for me. I can't stay here. I can't leave this room either."

I then explained the policy and he stared silently, possibly trying to figure out how to comfort me, but if I'd been him, I'd be counting the seconds until I could bolt out of that place.

"You don't have to stay. You can go to work, or home. There isn't even anywhere for you to sit." I told him.

"I will call Pam back and let her know where you are, but that you cannot have visitors."

"Okay."

He stroked my hand a little longer. "Do you need anything?" I shook my head.

"Let me know when they find you a room. Okay?"

"Okay," I cracked as I bit my lower lip and sniffed.

"I love you," he said as he kissed my cheek, lips, and forehead.

"I love you, too," I added as I lowered myself back down and he waved good-bye.

I was glad he'd gone. I could not explain how low I felt, or admit to him I'd run through the possible ways I could have killed myself during the night. Now, all I could do was wait. "I give up," I thought. Then, "no, dying would have been giving up. This was just giving in."

* * *

This time I remained awake, eyes closed, and listened to doors open and close, muffled voices in the hall, and was not surprised when the light came on and I heard a male say, "Ms. Edwards?"

I sat up and turned around to see a guy that was a little younger than I am holding the black plastic chair. "Hi. I'm Doctor So-and-So. I understand you're having a tough time. May I sit down?"

He came up to the foot of my bed, set the chair facing me, sat down and pulled out a pen. I noticed he had a clipboard, and he flipped the papers, looked up and said, "So are you seeing a doctor?"

I explained that I had been to my family physician but that the psychiatrist I'd seen before was out due to his own disease. "Oh, you were one of Terry's patients. Yeah, that's rough," he said, and I assumed he meant my doctor's personal life-threatening diagnosis, not my situation. "And you are taking Cymbalta?"

"Yes."

44

"For how long"

"Three weeks, but I don't think it is working yet."

He nodded. "It can take a while. Sometimes three months." He made a few notes and looked in my eyes. "I know you feel badly. It does get better."

I nodded.

He smiled softly, "I hear there is a room for you. We'll get you the help you need."

Thank goodness. I smiled half-heartedly in return, and tried to focus on the fact they'd found a room for me. I was going to get to leave this room.

"I'll let the nurse know you are ready to go as soon as the room is arranged," he added, shook my hand gently, told me it was nice meeting me and he added, "Take care, Mel," as he gathered himself and the chair and exited.

"It's going to be okay," I told myself, and I began to notice the various scratches and scuffs on the wall across from me for the first time.

* * *

Susan returned. "Your room is all set and we have called for transportation. Unfortunately, an ambulance cannot take you. We've called the police."

"I can't drive my car?"

"I'm sorry, but we have no way of supervising you if you do that. You'll have to have someone come get your vehicle later."

"Can my husband come and get me?"

"Not at this stage. The only approved transport is official public safety. For us, that's the police. They're just giving you a ride."

"Am I...under arrest?"

"No, but I guess I have to explain the law to you. The doctor at the facility will evaluate you, and you will need to stay as long as he feels is necessary for you to be safe on your own. It usually is a few days. Then, he will recommend to the judge to release you."

If my eyes weren't bulging out of my head before, I can only imagine what they looked like after she said that.

"Don't worry. You're going to get the best care possible. It'll be okay. We will let you know when the officer arrives to transport you."

Perhaps someone who had been on the wrong side of the law would know what was about to happen, but for a woman who'd only been pulled over for a rolling stop at a stop sign and one speeding infraction, which was dismissed by going to driving school for a day, I thought a nice officer would walk in, saying, "Okay, Ms. Edwards, we're ready to take you to your room," and off we'd go.

Instead, about a half hour later Susan stood in the hall and motioned her hand to my room, like a lady on a game show revealing a new car. In walked a balding, stout middle-aged male officer who said, "I'm Officer Grumpy, and my partner and I are here to bring you to Meadowview. If you don't give me a hard time, I won't put the cuffs on you."

Susan, the glory of Florence Nightingale herself, said, "Oh, that won't be necessary, I'm sure. She's been very cooperative."

Cooperative?! I came for help. I only wanted medication for my anxiety. I am supposed to be at work! I screamed in my head. Unable to cry or move, I sat in a state on the edge of my bed, feet dangling over the side.

Susan looked me in the eye, smiled a bit, handed me my clothes and turned to give Office Grumpy my plastic bag with my meds, ID, and car keys inside. She looked over her shoulder and said, "We'll be outside so you can change. When you're done, just open the door," and she did the game-show diva arm swoop again to usher the officer out.

She didn't shut the door all the way, but it was closed enough to give me privacy. I struggled with the cloth gown ties as my hands shook. I wanted a pair of scissors or a knife to cut the damned strings, but since that was not an option, I tried breathing until I could focus and get out of the gown without making a scene. I was going to be in the hands of the law in a minute, and I was smart enough to clam up and go along for the ride without incident.

Putting on my jeans, nightshirt, and sneakers was easier than removing the gown, and I opened the door slowly enough to not be eager, but quickly enough to appear solid instead of sketchy on my feet.

"Okay. Got everything?" Grumpy asked. "Yes, sir," I mumbled.

"Okay, my partner is outside. Let's go."

Luckily, his car was an unmarked vehicle, and he held open the back door for me to get in. His partner was already in the passenger seat and she was spitting chew juice into an old plastic soda bottle. I got in, tried not to gag over her tobacco habit, sat back, and Grumpy reminded me to put on my seatbelt. I wanted to laugh. I never knew cop cars had seatbelts in the back, and by the look of the two in front, I was amazed there was room for a computer to fit on the console between them.

Office Chew asked, "What's your address?"

I told her, and wondered why that mattered. They'd picked me up at the hospital, not at my home.

She typed it into the computer and called dispatch to let them know we were in route to Meadowview. I had no idea what or where Meadowview was, but I was guessing it was a mental hospital somewhere in town. I sat back trying to look relaxed and focused more on my lap and the laptop on the console than at them or outside. Most of the drive they were cracking jokes about how some of their colleagues would or would not conduct themselves at some conference in Vegas. Officer Chew assured Grumpy she was going to kick back and have a bit of fun while they were in town, regardless of what everyone else did.

As we drove along, I noticed we had crossed town and were headed incredibly close to my neighborhood, but instead of turning left down the main highway by the school, we continued to the right -- right toward my neighborhood, where I was supposed to be resting from working right now.

Geezum Crow! I go to the hospital because I hate my job, and then get brought to a facility within a few miles of the place? Karma is bitch! I thought.

Grumpy pulled into the Meadowview campus and I noticed 8" tall wrought iron fencing around the property, like some private hospital for the who's who of depressives. Was I living Girl, Interrupted? If so, was Angela Jolie in badly bleached hair in there?

The officers got out, and Chew handed Grumpy back my plastic bag. Guess she was no step-and-fetch-it female, I said to myself, but Officer Grumpy took it without word and marched to the front entrance. We stepped inside, with me as the pseudo-prisoner stuffing between the Navy blue sandwich bread.

The lobby of the facility looked to me more like a lawyer's foyer. It was small, dimly lit, dark carpet, with an office window for the receptionist, except no one was there to receive us. I relaxed a bit. Maybe this wouldn't be so bad after all.

We stood around a moment and the officers looked up and down the hallway leading away from reception while I stood in numb silence.

After a minute or two, a woman in general business attire said something about it not being visiting hours, but if there was something else she could help us.

Grumpy said, "We are delivering a patient."

The woman's tone immediately changed from hospitable to exasperation, "You came in the wrong door. You drove right past it. Go back outside and take a right. That's the door you were supposed to go to."

Chew and I turned and started to exit, and I thought, "Great. I don't even get to enter the front door."

We cut across the grass, passed a loading dock, and headed to the other door. When Chew pulled on it, we realized it was locked. By then Grumpy had caught up with us, and he saw the intercom located to the top left hand side of the door. He pressed the round gray button.

It buzzed and a voice said, "Can we help you?" Grumpy repeated, "We're here to deliver a patient." "One minute."

We stood about four feet from the door itself and a sweet-faced young woman came to the door, held up a finger indicating "one minute" and she dashed off to the left without attempting to let us in.

I stared at the grass, the bushes, the walls, and windows of the one story L-shaped brick building not the least bit concerned about the next stage. As far as I was concerned, I was at a place that could help me. In actuality, I was more concerned Grumpy and Chew might want to engage in small talk, so I stared at my shoes.

After standing outside in the mid-day sun for a few more minutes, I began to get a little warm. It was October, but temperatures still spiked regularly, and today was no exception. I thought about how close I was to my home, and my job, and felt doubly ashamed for being at this place. If I had not known they'd come after me if I ran, I might have bolted like a squirrel on the road, but that attempt would have been doomed, most certainly.

I was staring downward, reminding myself to breathe, when I heard keys in the door. It was locked from the inside, and it unsettled me that they could not open it nor could we enter without that key. My mind flashed to the infamous glove factory fire that killed the women workers trapped inside, but I shook it off and followed Grumpy inside while Chew brought up the rear.

The staff member with the key was not the same one who'd held up her finger in the doorway before. This one said I could have a seat and pointed at a cheap resin chair next to a long folding table. I didn't hesitate to take the opportunity, and I removed my coat.

Officers never seem to sit on the job, unless they're in their cars, I thought, as Grumpy and Chew waited for someone else to meet them and complete my transfer.

I stared at the carpet, noticing it was stained and aged, hoping no one would see my face and say, "Gee, aren't you Mel Edwards? Shouldn't you be at work right now?" I was in no mood to answer questions.

"Sorry, officers," a woman said.

I looked up. This was a third woman, thrusting a clipboard at Grumpy. He took it, and signed where she indicated. She asked if I had any belongings, and he passed the now-scrunched plastic bag to her. She thanked him, and walked them back to the door, which she unlocked for the officers to make their lawful, silent escape.

I swallowed hard as I heard the door shut, and the keys rattle as she turned the deadbolt. My heart beat like a rabbit crossing the road, and I wanted to run, but I was locked inside with no idea how to get out.

She walked toward me and said, "We'll be right with you. Everyone is either at lunch, or still walking back. As soon as Sheila is free, we'll have her grab someone else and they'll your intake."

There I was. Alone in the hallway of some facility that was supposed to have whatever was necessary to help me, locked inside, without a clue what to do. I had never felt so alone, and it did not occur to me that the woman with the key was unconcerned about leaving me in the hallway.

I closed my eyes, and wondered if I could muster a prayer, even a simple request. All that came to mind was, "Please, please help me," as tears began to run down my face.

INTAKE

In my right-hand coat pocket, I found a partially used tissue that was sufficient enough for me to blot my eyes, blow my nose, and make me appear what I imagined was reasonable. I did not see a trash can around, so back into the pocket it went. I remembered hearing once that Japanese people do a farmer's blow to shoot their snot out onto the earth, and find it disgusting that we carry ours around with us.

"Mel?" I looked up, and a sallow, be specked, middle-•-aged woman in beige scrubs that clashed with her skin tone said, "Come with me." She may have said her name, but I was too tired to pay close attention. I was not sure if she was a nurse or an aide. I simply stood, and followed her to the left, stood at the glass at the nurses" station. I knew that most hospitals did not have the nurses behind glass, and it seemed odd to me that this place was set up that way. We were buzzed in. She held the door for me, and we stepped into some kind of recreation room, as far as I could tell.

The door shut hard, and the lock clicked. Uncomfortable to now be behind a second door that I did not have the ability to open, I scanned the room to get my bearings. Close to the door, on the left was a clutch of heavy, walnut-stained furniture that could have come from a student union after it shed its 1970s vibe, but most of the cushions were missing. The seating was facing a mantel with a small flat screen TV mounted above it, but the device was off. In the far end were a couple of round tables that could fit into the dining area of an old folk's home, with vinyl seated metal chairs hastily shoved around them at a variety of angles. A few white people sat playing cards at the round tables, two older black patients were on the sofa's remaining cushions, staring into the air between them and the dark television screen, while a heavy-set, cocoa skinned woman with short-cropped hair, dressed in multiple layers of hospital gowns, and sock feet danced a solo, gentle twist as she hummed a tune I did not recognize. On the right was the nursing station, making a full 180 degrees of the turn from the outer hallway, with glass all around making the staff inside look like many varieties scrubs-clad fish, floating right and left around each other as they went around picking up binders, clipboards, and phones without ever interacting with each other.

I must have stopped entirely inside the door as I tried to take it all in, and my escort paused to look through a fistful of keys.

"We're headed in here, to the exam room," she indicated by using the folder in her left hand to point toward a door with a drawn window blind located just past the sofa. As she unlocked it, she said to a young white girl sitting in a blue fiberglass chair, "Where's Lisa?"

"The young woman looked up from her clipboard and said, "She's out with the smokers."

"Well, could you tell her I need her help with an intake?"

The young woman got up, and turned right, heading toward an exterior door.

It was nice to see I could go outside if I needed to, and I relaxed a bit.

"Come in and have seat, Mel," she said as she unlocked the exam room with her back still facing me. She flipped on the lights and I saw one of those old classroom plywood seats where the left arm becomes the desktop, so students can only step in or out from the right side. I walked to the right side, sat down sandwiched between the plywood arm and the hefty metal desk where she spread a folder. Then, she shut the door.

Three, I thought. That's the third door between me and the world. My rabbit heart skipped a beat, I was certain of it.

She sat at the desk beside the chair, face to the wall, and said nothing about me going to the Army green exam table as she opened the folder. She unwound the stethoscope from her neck, and I saw her white plastic nametag pinned to her uniform. Constance Jones, it stated, was a nurse, and I noticed that she did not look particularly pleased with her current task. In her defense, however, she also did not appear angry either. I wondered if she was tired as she checked my pulse, listened to my heart, and took my temperature. I was tired and I hoped I would get to go to my room soon.

Constance flipped through papers, made notes, and did not bother with small talk as she worked along. Meanwhile, I noticed a few wardrobe-style metal cabinets, tops piled high with boxes of gloves, and that the walls were a sickening tone of khaki. I wanted to pull my limbs and head into my turtle shell to wait out whatever Constance was working through, but she started to verify my name, address and other general information and I was forced to at least grunt out responses.

She pulled out a red folder and pointed out pamphlets and fliers as she began to explain the hospital policies. Apparently, the doctor was not in, and I would not see him until tomorrow morning. I was lucky, she said, because a patient named Andi had just checked out and I had insurance, so I would get her old room. She flipped to a section about visiting hours and told me she would need to know the names of the people who were allowed to visit.

That's it? My throat tightened as I realized I would not see my husband again until tomorrow night, and he still did not even know where I was. I nodded silently. What would I wear until then? Layers of hospital gowns like the dancing lady?

No. I will only wear them to bed. I will keep the clothes I came in on until my husband comes -• Tuesday night. I pinched my lips together and stared at the folder.

Three staccato knocks on the door sat me at attention. Nurse Jones rose to open it, and in came another middle-•-aged woman. "Sorry. I was also monitoring smoke break. The new girl isn't ready to do it on her own yet. What do you need?"

"This is Mel," Ms. Jones announced. "I need your help with the exam."

I presumed this was the woman that she had been looking for earlier. Nurse Jones turned to me and forced a little smile. "I am going to need you to take off your clothing so that we can examine you. I know it is cold in here, but you have to get down to your panties."

I slowly rose, and followed instructions as the nurse opened another page in my file that showed the front and back of a non-gender-specific humanoid shape, more like a thin gingerbread or toilet sign figure, and poised her pen as Lisa called out each pimple, scar, and blot on my flesh.

Is this what prison feels like? I wondered, hoping I would not also have to endure a cavity search.

"What's this?" Lisa said, as she pulled down the back of my underwear. "Is it a birth mark?"

"Yes," I squeaked.

Lisa ran her gloved hand over my back and said, "Nothing else significant," to Constance, and "You can get dressed again," to me.

I turned my back to them and tried to regain my dignity as I put my clothing back on. *They look at naked people all the time*, I thought as I bowed my head, *just not this person.*

Lisa then said she needed my picture and had me look at her while she hit the button on the instant camera. I nearly glared, but tried to soften my features.

"You can sit back down," she said as she placed the gray toned undeveloped film shot and the camera on the desk.

Nurse Jones said, "I'm good. Thanks."

Lisa said it was nice meeting me, and I mumbled "thanks" in return as she left.

Constance went back to the visitors list and said I could have toiletries but they had to be alcohol-•-free, and I could have a journal, or books brought in.

She then pointed out there was a schedule of activities and I would be in group A. "Group A, is highly functioning like you are. You'll be fine. When it is time for activities or meals, just line up at the door and we'll take you all together."

"Like I said before, you will have your own room. Lights out is 10 p.m.

Someone will check on you every fifteen minutes. You need to keep your bedroom door open. You will also need to keep your bathroom door open. Your room has its own bathroom, but it is in "A" wing, which is closed until just before bedtime. When you are not in meetings or doing activities, you will be in the main room outside this door. There is a pay phone, and if you want to make a call, let one of the attendants know at call time. You will be put on the list, and we ask that you keep calls to five minutes, as other people are waiting. Do you have any questions?"

I told her I did not think so, but she continued, "Group B will also be in the day room with you. If there is a problem let the staff know, and we will handle it. Okay?"

I agreed, and wondered if I could at least get something to eat.

"I have to ask you some more questions, but before I do that, have you eaten lunch?"

"I didn't even have breakfast," I whispered.

"We'll get you something," she said as she stood and opened the door. "Lisa?" She waited a moment and said, "Where did Lisa go now?"

A voice on the other side, perhaps the young woman from earlier, said something about medication time.

Nurse Jones barked, "I need a lunch for this patient. Can you make sure Lisa calls the kitchen and brings something for her?"

The voice agreed, and the nurse settled down a bit with a sincere sounding, "Thank you," as she shut the door and returned to her seat at the desk.

"Okay. I have several questions to ask you. Ready?" Without waiting for my answer, she started. "Have you ever attempted suicide?"

"No."

"Cut yourself?"

"No."

"Refused food?"

"No."

"Been overly-religious?"

"No."

"Had visions?"

"No."

"Forgotten where you were?"

And the questions continued until she completed them all. I was struck by the overly religious question. What did that mean?

"Okay, let's get your room assignment, and that lunch," she sighed.

Her hard edge was gone, and I chalked it up to being a stressful shift.

We stood, she opened the door and waited for me to leave the room first so she could lock it behind us.

In front of me was dancing woman, now arms reaching to the sky as she yelled "Talk to me, Jesus! Make me your instrument. Talk to me!"

"Phyllicia, Jesus is busy, why don't you go to your room and lie down for a nap?" Nurse Jones said. Then turning to me, "Go ahead and have a seat. I'll see about your lunch."

I picked one of the round tables and pulled out a chair, back to the phone, but facing the nurses" fishbowl and I watched Phyllicia as she told Constance that Jesus was coming for her, to use her as his instrument, and I guessed this is why I was asked if I were overly-religious.

A slender brown-haired man in a concert T-shirt and well-worn jeans said hi, but kept on his path toward the love seat with no cushions. He looked at the older black woman sitting on the sofa and asked if she knew when the cushions would be back.

The woman barked, "Who knows. If that fat pig hadn't pissed on them all, we'd have a place to sit. This place is disgusting. They ought to be ashamed of themselves!"

He didn't engage her further, and did his best to look comfortable sitting on the hard loveseat frame, minus any cushions.

So, this was to be home, I could not leave, I would not see the doctor today, and I wanted my husband. By now, I was too numb to cry or to care that I had not eaten, and I saw the clock said it was nearly 1 p.m.. *If I were at school, I'd be on detention duty*, I thought. *Instead, I'm now being detained.*

I looked around and wondered if they still did electroshock therapy, and envisioned Jack Nicholson's character from *One Flew Over the Cuckoo's Nest.*

PART TWO

UNDERSTANDING DEPRESSION
AND ASSISTING RECOVERY

I fully expect that people who buy books on depression want to know how they can help themselves, or someone they care about. Now that you know a bit more about how situational depression can manifest and the state of at least one type of treatment, the remainder of this book should help you answer "now what."

LET ME START BY PICKING APART MY JOURNEY.
THINGS I COULD HAVE CHANGED

1. Stopped beating myself up for my screw up.

2. Taken time for a more serious one-on-one conversation with each of my bosses to find a way to get the help that I so desperately needed to serve my students.

3. Stopped hiding from Mrs. Sopa after my mistake and one request for help, and rebuilt the trust that I had lost by my conduct error.

4. Resigned from teaching the year of my error.

5. Seen a therapist and a psychiatrist as soon as depression and Same Shit Satan walked into my life.

6. Reached out to those who had power to change the schooling system, become an advocate for the students, tried to stop social promotion, and excessive emphasis on standardized testing.

7. Continued my exercise routine to keep up my energy and reduce my stress.

8. Eaten more healthy foods. You know that kind that comes from the garden instead of the Franken-foods that list more chemicals than nutrients.

9. Woke up my husband the night of my emotional tsunami.

10. Called in sick instead of going to the ER, and seen my general practitioner or therapist, or both that day I was committed.

In other words, even though I am not to blame for being depressed, my actions and choices made it infinitely more difficult to recover.

Now that I feel like myself again, and depression is not running my emotional and mental responses, I wanted to share my story in hopes of saving at least one life, much the way anyone impacted by any horrific event would speak up and sound the alarm if confronted by the same situation again.

I had depression, a mental illness, but I am not crazy (a word that we should not use to dismiss those with mental diseases anyway). I was committed, but I'm certain that I did not belong in that institution. The hospital was filled with caring employees, and I know that most who worked there were doing the best that they could knowing full well their inadequate funding, less-than-optimal setup that mixed group A and B residents (who were both trying to retain dignity and recover) and the low number of human resources per patient.

Looking back upon everything, knowing what I know now, if I were as frustrated in a future position, I will use my voice and strong sense of injustice to speak up at work, defend myself/ my colleagues/our students against the system that was serving so few of us. I will fight against a canned standardized curriculum and excessive testing solely for data points. I will encourage parents to voice their rage with the policy makers, and students to share their concerns with their parents.

I am deeply grateful for all that went right while teaching in a situation where I felt so powerless and angry. Most of our students improved their overall performance, grew as young people, had genuine moments of insight and personal growth that I hope will be part of their core personas life-long. They made me proud, and even though they did not know why I'd been in the hospital that October, we found common ground to make the system as palatable as possible as they made their way to the "Promised Land of Passing". Students are the heart of education, and in my case, my whole reason for even wanting to be an educator.

As for my bosses, it is clear they were under immense pressure to follow the district, state and federal mandates, and they did so, regardless of their personal frustrations with the hand they were dealt. As far as I know, they each could have been as frustrated as I was, but they still showed up and did what they could.

My fellow educators who were just as beaten-down by the mandates showed up, jumped through more hoops than a circus dog, managed their personal and family lives and still supported each other. Several knew what I was going through and did their level best to bolster my vision of myself, and for that I am forever grateful.

I hold no one to blame, not even myself, for the journey I took down the rabbit hole because I honestly could not have fought my way out of a wet paper bag at the time of my depression. Now that I am back to my feisty self, complete with penchant for salty language, I am speaking up, have taken out my hypothetical hammer, and am ready to beat down the factors that contribute to the many-headed Hydra that is depression -- including causes, challenges with self and professional care, and erasing stigma.

DEPRESSION RUN AMOK

Depression, as you have read, can escalate to levels far more dire than those around us realize, all the way to the worst possible outcome: Suicide, because left unchecked, untreated, and unsupported that's where we could be headed. Robin Williams was not under the influence when he died. Spaulding Gray's temperament and health had changed dramatically as a result of an accident. Sylvia Plath, even after giving in to her illness, had the smarts to put rags around the kitchen door so gas would not reach her child. Norma Jean swallowed pills when she could no longer stomach her agony. Decades apart, two men in my hometown waited until their children were in school, while another highly esteemed man in the Bible Belt plunged his gun into his gut in a parking lot as friends, including a well-meaning preacher who knew him personally, looked on and begged him to change his mind, if not for himself, at least for his estranged wife and children who were inside the church. The cobalt thread of unbearable pain and sadness draws these stories together. In our inability to understand we tie them into the same, knotted category. Trying to connect each incident is like saying all car collisions are identical when in reality only our terminology links them. We are each different bodies and minds, with individual needs. Shouldn't our treatment solutions be unique, too?

Over seven billion people are on Earth, and as I write, I stare at the world population clock to see today's birth rate has already topped 13,000 and those who have passed away are just under 10,000, from all possible causes combined. Environmental resources are dwindling; human impact is accelerating. I can't help but note the irony that saving lives could, possibly, lead to the planets" demise. As for the realists, who wonder why preventable death matters, I tell you that I am a romantic, and I believe saving lives could change the world for the better. Not so certain? Okay, as food for thought, I'll direct you to my Pinterest board on defeating depression and anxiety, to the pin that shows famous faces of depression as a graphic created by ifred.org.

In regards to how I became depressed, there are genuine underlying medical reasons, which I won't go into depth explaining, but even if it were entirely psychosomatic, what person has the right to judge me, save myself? Certainly, we have no business judging each other, and yet we do it. All of us do it -- day after day. This leads to stigma, shame and helps no one. So, I am asking us all to stop. Suspend categorizing and finger pointing. Open each of our selves up, and prepare to see the truth of clinical, life-threatening, ever-present depression. It is a disease that comes unbidden. Of the 350 million worldwide sufferers, most of us are survivors for our "time" when old age or other circumstances call.

If you have never experienced something as basic as the Sunday blues, it may be hard to grasp how any high-achieving, success-oriented person can end up locked in a hospital when all she did was ask for a help because her medicine had not yet kicked in. You may question how someone else -- a person who never misses work or school -- could suddenly lose his grasp on daily routine, and be drained of all strength, needing immediate transportation to a mental health facility. For you, depression exists in literature, film, and perhaps in a "once-in- a-lifetime" nightmare. But in reality, the despair of depression grips roughly one in five minds. That is one heck of a lot of us that you ought to try to understand a bit better if for no other reason than to keep yourself informed.

Medications, therapies, and denial all contribute to the rise and fall of any disease, but I believe that truth, understanding, and connections can suppress the impact of many diseases. The negative loneliness of depression thrives in darkness, and softens in the light of day.

Depression can be deadly, and treatment is not telling someone to "get over it," or to "snap out of it." Saying a prayer and singing a happy song won't transform brain chemistry. Every patient is different, but understanding and unity can save lives, build community and change someone's world. Likewise, speaking about it will not lead someone to take his or her own life, and can open his or her eyes and hearts to the good in you for reaching out and in the world for having assistance.

It is my hope that the facts, resources and philosophies presented in the second half of this book are an opening or a window that allows everyone to realize illness is as individual as the patient and treatment comes in whatever forms are available. For better options, we must remove the stigma, ask for and expect quality care from our communities - regardless of income or geographic location.

Spread the word that no one needs to suffer in silence, and if you like what you have read here, please visit my Amazon author page and leave a positive review. Believe it or not, your honest opinion can help others decide to purchase this book, and open a new world of resources for themselves. In other words, you can help save lives by continuing the conversation, erasing stigma, and supporting those who need it most.

Oh, and if you do not like this book, send me an email with one specific action that I can take to serve you better. (And no, Trolls, "go kill yourself" isn't an option.) It is my pleasure to assist my readers and help make the world a better place.

CHALLENGE OF ONE TO FOUR MILLION

According to the World Health Organization (WHO), approximately one in five children and adolescents have a mental disorder, and in the low to middle income nations, there is as few as one child psychiatrist for every one to four million patients. Read that again - one child psychiatrist for everyone one to four million patients. (http://www.who.int/features/factfiles/mental_health/mental_heal th_f acts/en/

This fact led the WHO to declare 2012 a year to focus upon mental health service around the world, and that year on Mental Health Day (October 10th of each year), Secretary-General Ban Ki-Moon (b. Korea 13 June 1944) released a press statement with the headline, "Depression No Matter for Experts Alone" and went on to add that action is needed by citizens in general to "relieve related stigma."

As an adult in a higher income nation, I cannot imagine walking up to a child and telling him or her to shut up and not tell anyone he or she is ill. Yet, that's exactly what we have done to ourselves, and our loved ones, for centuries the world over. Silence is not treatment or a cure, and hiding in shame does nothing to help the sick, desperate and equally important.

I am fortunate enough to know people who have secured an astonishing array of medical services to save their children's lives, give them constant care, and change their mortality rate because such services exist in our nation. However, at this moment, I have yet to have a single conversation with any parent in a social setting about what mental health care they have provided for themselves or their children. This leads me to wonder if these same vigilant parents are either embarrassed about the care their children need, or if they are struggling, as I did, trying to find adequate care by a qualified provider to yield satisfactory and manageable outcomes to serve themselves and their families.

In fact, it was not until after I found myself involuntarily hospitalized that I had a real conversation with my own friends, colleagues, and family members about mental health care beyond a simple admission of some needing antidepressants. Several have sworn me to silence not to tell of their own disorders, including bipolar two -- something that I had never even heard of until not one but three friends confessed their own diagnosis to me. So here I was, recovering from my own depression, surrounded by others who have been suffering silently, and all I could think of was, "Why is it okay to sell pink ribbons and wear T-shirts emblazoned with 'Save the Ta-Tas' but not 'Sorry, My Brain Doesn't Want to Play Nice Today' on them?"

Will joining mental health support groups change our world? For some of us, it just might. One organization I've been introduced to is the National Alliance on Mental Illness (NAMI). NAMI is a non-profit and is worth investigating for yourself. You'll see they have warning signs, treatment options, mental health by the numbers and their Stigma-Free pledge. In looking at their infographic for the United States, I confirmed that suicide is the 10th leading cause of death in my nation, as noted by the American Journal of Psychiatry and U.S. Surgeon General's Report, 1999. You can download and see the entire infographic here (https://www.nami.org/NAMI/media/NAMI-Media/Infographics/General-MHFacts-9-23-15.pdf)

Go ahead. I'll wait.

Now that you've seen a few famous faces, heard a few statistics, and checked out things for yourself, I hope you will agree that something needs to be done to help people live healthier lives and be treated with dignity.

WHAT CAUSES DEPRESSION?

Anger turned inward, as noted by Julie and Saul, my former counselors (not their real names, by the way), is one theory for the cause of depression. Enduring chronic pain also leads to the loss of resiliency. Those who are chronically bullied and marginalized, such as members of the LGBTQIQ communities are at high risk for depression. People of color are at risk in America because the playing field is not level for them, still, in spite all the advancements of the past fifty years. Soldiers with PTSD and people who have suffered traumatic brain injuries, including childhood concussions are also at risk. Adults whose whole identity is wrapped around a job or life role they no longer hold live with depression. When a person feels there is absolutely no way out of a situation that she or he cannot control, sometimes the only relief that person can imagine is a final exit from life itself.

Feeling of futility, weakness and despair are real. I am not a doctor or therapist, and I certainly don't advocate anyone living my path. I am laying it bare so that perhaps you, or someone you love, will see that watching a funny film, changing a job or other relationship by itself will not resolve clinical depression. The mind is a complicated instrument, and our biology complex. Do not think finding or employing only one solution will bring you or anyone else to perfect mental health.

What Do We Do?

For some sufferers medication can help, once it kicks in, if the side effects do not outweigh the benefits. Cognitive therapy and life changes give patients some power back. Talking about our anger, powerlessness and frustrations also helps, which is why I was willing to tell my whole truth. Even now that I'm better, and stronger, nothing scares me more than telling everyone I know how I experienced depression, and contributed to it, but it is the only way I have left to let all of my anger go. Sharing it is not the same as speaking it into existence, and the only way to get where I want to go is to walk through the fear and do it anyway. So if you want to fight to take away my teaching licenses, go on with your bad self. You have no power over me, and if that's the best use of your time, you're sicker than I ever was.

My major depression has lived within me long enough. As I release my truth, I half-expect a pack of wolves to gather around and rip the flesh from my bones in an effort to silence me and keep the status quo. I expect lost friendships, burned career bridges, and a long line of folks at my doorstep expecting me to save them, too. I cannot save anyone, except perhaps myself, and trust me when I say that at the depths of a major depressive event I could not even do that. Now that I'm stronger, I can listen, witness and let anyone who cares to hold my truth in his or her hands and remind his/herself that this disease is not our spirit, our legacy, or our hearts. We are so very much more, and we deserve a fighting chance to prove it to ourselves most of all.

If you want to join the positive movements that fight to break down barriers, lift up survivors and prevent suicide, the resources at the end of this book can lead you to many solutions that may be a fit for your level of interest in activism. There are community walks -- such as the Out of Darkness Walks sponsored by the American Foundation of Suicide Prevention (https://www.afsp.org/out-of-the-darkness-walks), legislative initiatives such as the Jason Flatt Act (http://jasonfoundation.com/about-us/jason-flatt-act/) which focuses upon training teachers and support groups for families and others who have been left behind after a loved ones suicide (http://www.suicide.org/suicide-support-groups.html), and more if you do the research.

MENTAL HEALTH AND EMPLOYEES

Anyone who has ever taken a psychology class probably has some rudimentary knowledge about what stress is caused by and what it looks like. For example, there are good stressors (eustress) like one might expect if you hit the lottery, and negative stressors (distress) such as being chased by a vicious animal. When faced with negative stress, we can either stand our ground or fight the stressor or high tail it out of there. This is known as fight or flight response.

Stress is unavoidable in daily life, but can be minimized by having a comfortable, relatively safe atmosphere to live within. For me, that means a clutter-free household, keeping up with regular tasks (laundry, dishes, paying bills on time), making enough money to meet my commitments, and having sufficient funds to enjoy life. When my basic needs are not being met, my level of distress rises. However, even when all of the things that I can control are going well, life can hand me distressing events that I may not have any control of whatsoever. When I'm healthy, I can take a moderate amount of distressing events and manage to cope through the serpentine path they wind. When I'm already ill, my basic needs are unmet, my emotional well is running on fumes, that's when distress becomes less manageable and, in time, my ability to cope diminishes exponentially and I eventually feel depressed. That type of depression I personally call survival mode and too long in survival leads to a major depressive episode in my life. When my emotional, mental, and physical reserves are abundant I have set myself up for continued success, health and am able to avoid major depression. Does that make sense?

PLEASE ALLOW ME TO GUIDE YOU THROUGH SOME QUESTIONS ABOUT YOUR OWN COMFORT ZONES AND HEALTH NEEDS.

What is a nourishing, pleasing diet for you that will leave you feeling energetic and satisfied?

How much sleep and downtime do you need to feel ready to greet the day with a can-do attitude?

What is your idea of a fun time that leaves you seeking to play or do more?

Who do you turn to with you best news?

Where can you go when you are faced with devastation, destruction, or illness?

When you've had a day full of uncontrollable setbacks, how to do drop back and regroup?

Do you have a crutch -- such as alcohol, drugs, or food -- that you use to soothe yourself when "shit happens"?

Is there a higher power or respected source that you turn to when it seems that nothing is going right?

Do you have access to people who are trusted confidants who will tell you honestly when they're concerned about your health, safety, and success?

How close (both physically and emotionally) are you to your relatives?

If a major environmental disaster were to strike your home, your community, or your job, how would you build yourself and your life back up to match your needs?

Who, or what, makes you feel wanted, capable and successful in your daily life?

Are you surrounded by people (as well as circumstances) that give you hope, and make you energized? Or does your daily routine tap your reserves and leave you feeling drained?

If you were suddenly sidelined, due to circumstances beyond your control, who would step up and help you out -- even if that meant asking for assistance?

Have you learned to ask for help without feeling ashamed or guilty?

If you truly have taken time with these questions, you should have a clear idea of the strength you have to hold you up, keep you moving in a direction of your choosing and catch you when you fall. Notice, I did not say catch you IF you fall. No one is strong all the time. Realize that there will be low ebbing moments in your energy and have a plan to deal with it. As one of my former supervisors told me, always have a plan B, and expect to always use it.

FIVE WAYS TO HELP SOMEONE FACE DEPRESSION

1. Don't give trite or glib responses to someone about their depression.

This is a life-threatening disease, and needs to be treated as such. I expect that you would never play a song like "Don't Worry Be Happy" to cure someone with lymphoma. Certainly, depression is a mood disorder but playing a film, a visit by a clown or giving one hug will not make it vanish. Depression isn't a bad moment, or day, but several days, usually week after week.

2. Listen. Acknowledge. Seek understanding.

You are not asked or expected to fix depression. Instead, listen to what pains the person and then state your understanding in return. *Once you understand, however, and it is clear that depression is present, absolutely go to step #3!*

3. **Encourage people with any medical ailment to seek solutions from a qualified professional that they trust and respect.**

In other words, have them get a referral - immediately. For example, if the person in your life who is suffering from depression is an atheist, seeing a minister will not help, and no matter how kind and well- qualified the spiritual leader may be, whatever is said during a session will be met with resistance if it is heard at all. Likewise, if an ill person does not trust medications going to the family doctor may cause the patient to become upset and angry and not follow prescribed orders or medical therapies. In the end, more suffering is created and no solution is reached.

If the person you're encouraging will not make the move on his/her own, you may be morally and legally obligated to call for help for them, depending upon your profession, and their level of distress.

Now I bet you're thinking, but he/she trusts me. If I do that, I'll lose his/her trust.

Look at my story. Was I ticked off that I was committed? You betcha! Could it have saved my life if I really was going to harm myself? Yes. It certainly gave me something to think about (the nasty place and lack of real treatment and support) instead of being stuck in the racing, irrational thoughts about my job and my future.

As a result, if I had a situation where I felt I needed to contact authorities, for myself or someone else, I would. I would rather have an angry friend than a dead one any day. And, yes, I did swear I could never go back into such an institution on my own… but let's be realistic: One live Mel is better than a dead one. Period.

4. Offer help in an area where you're highly skilled and interested in doing so.

I'm a firm believer that people with depression are often so bereft of energy that even undertaking the most simple of tasks is nearly impossible -- including meeting their own basic needs of bathing, eating, resting. If you want to do something that really does help offer to run a bath for a friend, take the kids out for a bit while your loved one rests, bring over a simple meal and share it. You don't need to be a superhero and take over their entire treatment plan or make it your mission in life to turn them around single-handedly (which is a recipe for your own emotional downturn once you are exhausted and spent of any energy reserves that you have).

Remember, not all depressed people are suicidal. Sometimes being numb and unable to muster action is the extent of the suffering. This goes back to step 2. If you listened well, you will know what your friend or loved one needs most from you that you are also willing to do.

5. Do not pressure or nag.

Many with depression are already beating themselves up mentally for being ill, feeling useless and unable to cope. Giving deadlines, telling them to get back to work/workouts/doing a hobby or completing tasks that need attention in an effort to get the patient on track will only backfire and create resentment. Instead, go back to step 2 and listen to see if he/she is interested in doing any of these things at the moment. If the patient's desire exists that is the time to support him or her by offering assistance -- but only if it doesn't create a sense of obligation or resentment. Nagging will not fix anything, and whining about "well I helped you, why aren't you better yet" when you show up will not help the situation either.

CLOSED

FOR SANITY
RECONSTRUCTION.

--MEL EDWARDS

RESOURCES FOR MENTAL HEALTH ASSISTANCE, EDUCATION, AND SUPPORT

Suicide Hotlines - International Numbers
http://www.suicide.org/international-suicide-hotlines.html

Suicide Hotlines for Each U.S. State
http://www.suicide.org/suicide-hotlines.html

SUICIDE PREVENTION RESOURCES

American Foundation for Suicide Prevention
http://www.afsp.org/

The Jason (Flatt) Foundation
http://jasonfoundation.com/

The Jed (Satow) Foundation
http://www.jedfoundation.org/

NAMI, National Alliance on Mental Illness -
National site (*Note: Individual state sites also connected to national pages*)
http://www.nami.org/

Organization for People of Color Against Suicide
http://www.ncsp.org/nopcas.html

Suicide Awareness Voices of Education

http://www.save.org/

Stop a Suicide Today

http://www.stopasuicide.org/

Substance Abuse and Mental Health Administration

http://www.samhsa.gov/

Suicide Prevention Resource Center

http://www.sprc.org/

The Trevor Project (LGBTQ)

http://www.thetrevorproject.org/

U.S. Department of Veteran's Affairs

http://www.va.gov/

Yellow Ribbon (Suicide Prevention Plan)

http://yellowribbon.org/

SUPPORT ORGANIZATIONS
FOR PEERS, FRIENDS AND FAMILIES

Active Minds

http://www.activeminds.org/

Depression and Bipolar Support Alliance

http://www.dbsalliance.org

National Mental Health Consumer's Self-Help Clearinghouse

http://www.mhselfhelp.org/

National Empowerment Center

http://www.power2u.org/

National Coalition for M
ental Health Recovery

http://ncmhr.org/

STAR (Support Technical Assistance Resources) Center

http://www.consumerstar.org/

To Write Love On Her Arms

https://twloha.com/

You are Not
Weak if
You Ask
For Help
or Receive It.
--Mel Edwards

TRAINING RESOURCES

Mental Health Screening - Youth Program

https://mentalhealthscreening.org/programs/youth/sos

QPR (Question Persuade Refer)

http://www.qprinstitute.com/

State and Community Resources - Courtesy of Suicide Prevention Resource Center (*click on your state on map for details*)

http://www.sprc.org/states

Youth Suicide Prevention School-Based Guide

http://theguide.fmhi.usf.edu/

MEL'S COLLECTED RESOURCES FOR DEFEATING DEPRESSION AND ANXIETY

Depression and Anxiety Smackdown

https://www.pinterest.com/msmeledwards/depression-and-anxiety-smackdown/

Live Your Truth

https://www.pinterest.com/msmeledwards/live-your-truth/

Success Creation

https://www.pinterest.com/msmeledwards/success-creation/

Up, Ready, Move 30 Day Challenge

https://www.pinterest.com/msmeledwards/up-ready-move-30-day-challenge/

Zen and Meditations

https://www.pinterest.com/msmeledwards/zen-and-meditations:

SMACKING DOWN

{ DEPRESSION }

AND ANXIETY IS

{ A CONTINUOUS }

BATTLE FOR MANY.

{ CELEBRATE }

THE VICTORIES

OF EACH HOUR AND DAY.

AIM TO WIN THE WAR.

--MEL EDWARDS

DEPRESSION SMACKDOWN SYSTEM

Get up by 6 a.m. on weekdays, and by 7:30 a.m. on weekends.

Workout every day - even if it is only a 2.5 mph saunter on the treadmill for half an hour in total.

Take a multi-vitamin. (My depression came in part due to incredibly low vitamin levels.)

Eat something green every day --- usually a salad as my dinner.

Nap, if needed, on weekend days.

Go to bed early, even if I have taken a nap.

Wear a pedometer to track my activity -- because it is more objective than my recollection of how active I have been.

Listen to podcasts from people who are doing what I admire or would like to emulate.

Pay down debts, because debt made me a slave to a work situation that led to worsened depression.

Get rid of stuff that I do not need or appreciate enough -- opting for more of a minimalist lifestyle -- because stuff did not make me less depressed.

Speak up against things that eat at my soul.

Speak up for the good people and things in the world.

Admit my mistakes, and forgive myself. Then move onward, looking forward.

Live my life MY way: #The Bold Way.

Do no harm.

A FEW BONUS TIPS

I have some friends who suffer from Seasonal Affective Disorder. For them, having full-spectrum light in the home helps keep the blues away. I use an OTT light on my desk and have a home-made low-budget chandelier in my work room with a natural light CFL bulb. It is the brightest room in the home all day, and that makes me happier to be writing there.

I rarely watch TV and steer as clear as possible from the so-called news as I can. I call the news "the body count report" (and have since long before my depression) because it seems to me sensationalism rules in news broadcasting today, and most stations that used to give an hour of news each morning, noon, and evening now run non-stop with more editorial than facts. I'm better off looking online for anything I want to know, and it keeps my mind clear to make my own assessments of things instead of being a parrot for a talking head.

Third, related to not watching the news is realizing that because I can only control what I do in the world there is no reason to watch endless hours of others" battles. I am aware of gun-related violence, domestic violence, homelessness, hunger, war, refugees, immigration challenges and more, but until I can fix it there is no reason to listen to the next set of political pundits put on a show about what they would do if they were in charge. I can, however, decide if I want to own a gun, work at a domestic shelter, give to charities, and help people one-on-one.

Finally, I want to address personal identity. We each decide what we want to be known for in this life through our choices, passions, education, and actions. The way we were born and what life handed us in our youth, or the struggles of our nation (or its economy or our businesses) all impacts who we are on a variety of levels. However, we are all multi-faceted beings. If a marriage fails, we are not failures at all relationships. If a job does not work out, we can either change careers or become entrepreneurs. If we must move to live a safe life of our choosing, we can build again. Do not let one circumstance define you, as I had let one word tear down my self-worth so far that I became life- threateningly ill.

I am an educator, storyteller, and author. I hope that there is at least one thing in this book that has helped you understand depression is a collection of experiences and moments, not one's entire life or identity. I will probably never return to the traditional K-12 classroom because I am not an actor. I do not teach by script. I teach people what they need to be successful at whatever outcome they're aiming for in life. I rather see the entire nation refuse to take standardized tests than to teach to one, and I will never believe that shoving kids into longer classes will make them stronger students.

If you are looking to live on the bright side of life, make a difference in this world not only for yourself but for others, and are willing to buck the status quo to let your star shine, please join me. Live YOUR way, The Bold Way, and become a defeater of depression in the process.

NOW WHAT?

Here you are at the end of *Depression Smackdown.*

You have been given all you need for the following outcomes:

*Realize anyone can become depressed.

*Accept that most things in life we cannot control, but even so, we can control our responses to those events. Usually. (Remember, an ill, tired, depressed, and angry person will never have the same response as a healthy, strong, well-rested, grounded person.)

*Understand that depression does not have to be a death sentence. (If over three million have the disease in the United States, there are many who are coping, defeating, and moving to a place of health and strength.)

*Honor the truth that a healthy life is a daily set of choices centered around your own self-care, and these self-care choices are elements that you have immense control over.

*State there is no reason to be ashamed for suffering from any disease, including depression or any other mental illness.

*Remember, that with millions of people worldwide who face mental illness on a daily basis, you are not alone.

BE A POSITIVE FORCE

If obtaining, maintaining, and promoting mental health is important to you, get involved. Reach out to like-minded people (and, no, that's not meant to be a joke, even if it is a pun). Take action. Be a positive force in your universe.

QUOTES FOR
DEFEATING DEPRESSION AND ANXIETY

Quotes help me, still, and keep me moving along the way.

Here are a baker's dozen that I believe you'll appreciate, too.

"There are only two ways to live your life. One is as though nothing is a miracle.

The other is as though everything is a miracle."
-Albert Einstein

"Never be afraid to fall apart because it is an opportunity to rebuild yourself the way you wish you had been all along."
-Rae Smith

"Don't die with your music still inside you. Listen to your intuitive inner voice and find what passion stirs your soul."
-Wayne Dyer

"Never run back to what broke you."
-Unknown

"You cannot find peace by avoiding life."
- Unknown

"If you live for people's acceptance, you will die by their rejection."
-Lecrae

"You change your life by changing your heart."
- Max Lucado

"When you follow your bliss, doors will open for you that wouldn't have opened for anyone else."

- Joseph Campbell

"Happiness does not depend upon what you have or who you are. It solely relies on what you think."
  -Buddha

"You can let hate, anger, and animosity eat away at your, or you can let it go, and begin again."
  -Leon Brown

"I hope that you live a life that you are proud of. If you find that you are not, I hope that you find the strength to start all over again."
  -F. Scott Fitzgerald

"Your greatest gift to your family and friends is yourself - your relaxed, happy, and fully-present self."
  - Jonathan Lockwood Huie

"Become loyal to your inner-most truth.
Follow the way when all others abandon it.
Walk the path of your own heart."
  -Unknown

If you've liked what I have shared here, and my mission to be a life-long defeater of depression, please visit:

www.msmeledwards.com to team up with me for a better future for all. Together, we can change the world. I know we can.

OTHER BOOKS BY MEL EDWARDS

- The Bold Way: Find, Claim, Live Your Truth
- The Bold Way Workbook: Drilling Down to Your Truth
- La Manera Audaz (Spanish)
- As Spirit Moves Me: Poems and Photographs of Everyday Life

ABOUT MEL EDWARDS

Mel is a first-generation college graduate with several degrees, certifications and licenses. In addition to being an author and educator, she is a professional speaker, and storyteller.

For fun and relaxation she participates in visual and performing arts, and dreams of -- one day -- having her very own HBO Special. (Do they ever do those anymore? As you can tell, she doesn't watch much TV, so she doesn't know. If HBO went out of business, she wouldn't know that, either. Anyway, don't tell her if her dream is impossible.)

Mel lives in Indianapolis, Indiana with her husband, and their 17-year old toy poodle, Petey, and for the record, Mel's feeling much better these days.